D0945650

The 500 Hidden Secrets of
TORONTO

INTRODUCTION

There is one poignant moment in recent Toronto history that perfectly represents the beauty of this city. If you google 'Syrian refugee, gay pride Toronto' you will find a photo of a Syrian refugee holding a Canadian rainbow flag, marching in his first pride parade. In this city you are free to be yourself. You are safe and accepted regardless of race, religion, or sexuality. Here, the stereotype of Canadians as kind and welcoming people holds true.

Toronto may not be a city with a long history, but it is rich in experiences. The goal of this guide is to encourage users to step away from the shadow of the CN Tower and to explore beyond the cliché of Canadians in plaid shirts and moose on the highway.

We are a cosmopolitan city with a vibrant music scene, a multitude of festivals and great ethnic restaurants. The boasting film industry has given rise to the nickname 'Hollywood of the North'. Indigenous culture is alive and thriving, and many of the places in this book invite you to reconsider your own identity.

The book and its maps are organized by areas rather than neighbourhoods. Toronto contains too many cultural neighbourhoods to name individually and do them each justice, so in true Canadian fashion a compromise was found. Within each area there are new secrets waiting to be discovered.

HOW TO
USE THIS BOOK?

This book lists 500 things you need to know about Toronto in 100 different categories. Most of these are places to visit, with practical information to help you find your way. Others are bits of information that help you get to know the city and its inhabitants. The aim of this guide is to inspire, not to cover the city from A to Z.

The places listed in the guide are given a number and include an address and area. The area and number allow you to find the locations on the maps at the beginning of the book: first look for the map of the corresponding area (for example Downtown or Midtown), then look for the right number. A word of caution however: these maps are not detailed enough to allow you to find specific locations in the city. You can obtain an excellent map from any tourist office or in most hotels, and of course you can locate the addresses on your smartphone.

Please bear in mind that cities change all the time. The chef who hits a high note one day may be uninspiring on the day you happen to visit. The hotel ecstatically reviewed in this book might suddenly go downhill under a new manager. Or the bar recommended as one of 'the locals' 5 favourite spots for a drink' might be empty on the night you visit. This is obviously a highly personal selection. You might not always agree with it. If you want to leave a comment, recommend a spot or reveal your favourite secret place, please follow @500hiddensecrets on Instagram or Facebook and leave a comment. And of course it's always a good idea to visit our website *www.the500hiddensecrets.com,* where you'll find lots of new content, freshly updated info and travel inspiration.

THE AUTHOR

Erin FitzGibbon is an artist, photographer, writer, and a bit of a chameleon. She studied English Literature and Creative Writing at Acadia University in Nova Scotia, followed by a bachelor's in Education at the University of Western Ontario. She drifted away from the creative world for a while, but was suddenly drawn back to art and writing after the death of her son. Discovering photography along the way, she forged a new path forward.

Erin is a resident writer for the popular blog Digital Photography School *(digital-photography-school.com/author/erinfitzgibbon)*. She works as a freelance writer for a variety of different websites, blogs and magazines, and teaches courses in art and photography in the Greater Toronto Area.

Special thanks are due to the multitude of people who supported Erin through the marathon that was the creation of her first book. People shared more locations and ideas than there was room for – another 500 secrets could easily be added. Special recognition goes out to Mo who calmly reminded her to focus and keep working. To Brad for all his suggestions and helpful edits. Thank you to Karly, David, Tammy and her boys for acting as assistants at photoshoots. Thanks to all at Luster Publishing for your support, especially Dettie and Katya. This series is an amazing resource for every traveller.

TORONTO

overview

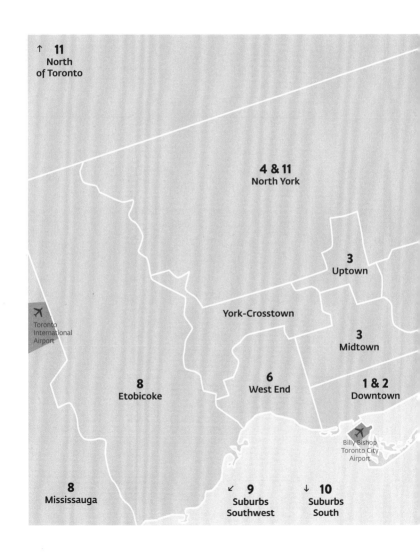

↑ **11**
North
of Toronto

4 & 11
North York

3
Uptown

York-Crosstown

Toronto
International
Airport

3
Midtown

8
Etobicoke

6
West End

1 & 2
Downtown

Billy Bishop
Toronto City
Airport

8
Mississauga

↙ **9**
Suburbs
Southwest

↓ **10**
Suburbs
South

7
Scarborough

4
East York

5
East End

Lake Ontario

Map 1
DOWNTOWN
NORTH

Map 2
DOWNTOWN
SOUTH

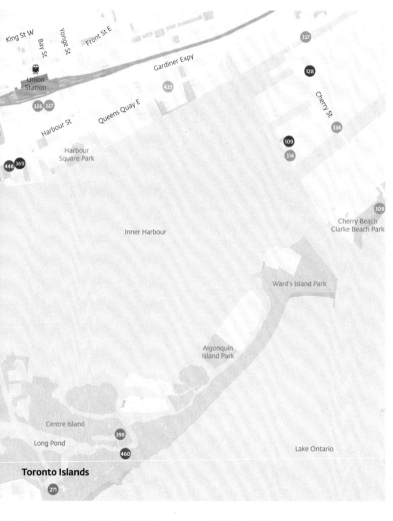

King St W

Bay St

Yonge St

Front St E

Union Station

Gardiner Expy

Queens Quay E

Harbour St

326 327

433

Harbour Square Park

448 469

Inner Harbour

337

128

Cherry St

336

109

314

309

Cherry Beach
Clarke Beach Park

Ward's Island Park

Algonquin
Island Park

Centre Island

Long Pond

398

460

Lake Ontario

Toronto Islands

271

Map 3
UPTOWN and
MIDTOWN

EAT – **DRINK** – SHOP – FASHION – BUILDINGS – DISCOVER – **CULTURE** – CHILDREN – SLEEP – **WEEKEND** – RANDOM

Map 4
NORTH YORK *and*
EAST YORK

Map 5
EAST END

Map 6
WEST END

EAT — **DRINK** — SHOP — FASHION — BUILDINGS — DISCOVER — **CULTURE** — CHILDREN — SLEEP — **WEEKEND** — RANDOM

Map 7
SUBURBS EAST
SCARBOROUGH

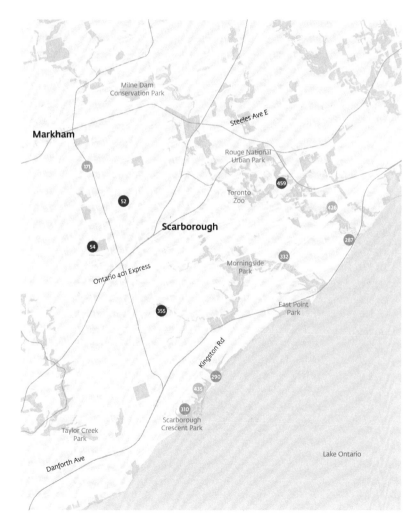

Map 8

SUBURBS WEST

MISSISSAUGA and ETOBICOKE

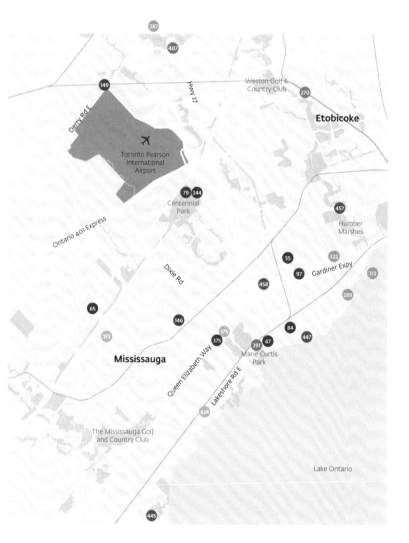

Map 9
SUBURBS SOUTHWEST

OAKVILLE, DUNDAS *and* HAMILTON

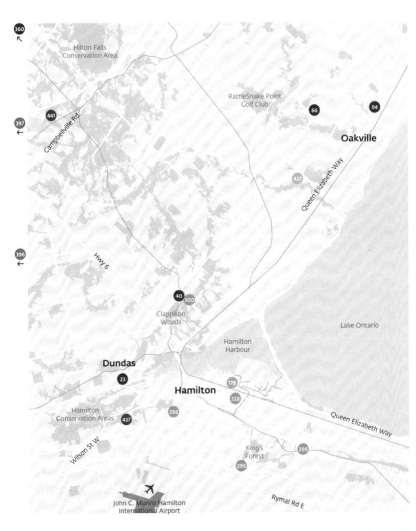

Map 10
SUBURBS SOUTH
JORDAN, NIAGARA and
NIAGARA-ON-THE-LAKE

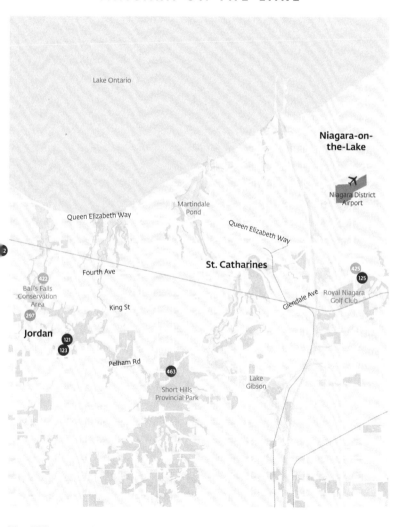

Map 11
NORTH OF TORONTO

Lake
Huron

Lake Huron /
Georgian Bay

Hwy 26

Hwy 21

454 Southampton

Eugenia
Lake
465

Hwy 10

Hwy 6

Hwy 9

Hwy 89

Luther
Lake

Lake Huron / Georgian Bay

Lake Simcoe

95
Barrie

429

Hwy 27

Hwy 400

Hwy 89

462

Newmarket
22

Hwy 48

Mono
124 280

Hwy 9

Richmond Hill
147
148

Vaughan
370 321
442 399

424 311
Caledon

North York
403
285 374 174 126
356
44

464 443

EAT — DRINK — SHOP — FASHION — BUILDINGS — DISCOVER — CULTURE — CHILDREN — SLEEP — WEEKEND — RANDOM

85 PLACES TO EAT OR BUY GOOD FOOD

———

The 5 best places to find a
PEAMEAL SANDWICH

1 **CAROUSEL BAKERY**
AT: ST. LAWRENCE
MARKET
**92-95 Front St E,
Upper Level 42
Downtown** ①
+1 416 363 4247
*stlawrencemarket.
com/vendors/vendor_
detail/56*

Carousel Bakery is located in the famous St. Lawrence Market. They've been serving up peameal sandwiches for over 30 years. During busy lunch hours you might not find a place to sit. While at the market try out Paddington's Pump. They also boast about having the best peameal sandwiches.

1 CAROUSEL BAKERY

2 PATRICIAN GRILL

219 King St E
Downtown ①
+1 416 366 4841
patriciangrill.com

Patrician Grill is a family-owned sixties-style diner. It's a down-to-earth local hotspot. The decor, the food and the atmosphere make this restaurant a welcoming place to enjoy a meal. If you're not into bacon sandwiches, there are lots of other options you can sample.

3 AVENUE OPEN KITCHEN

7 Camden St
Downtown ①
+1 416 504 7131
aveopenkitchen.ca

Avenue Open Kitchen is a classic Canadian greasy spoon. The prices are extremely reasonable and you get lots of food for your dollar. The peameal sandwich is served on rye bread with lots of fries on the side. You might also try the Montreal Smoked Meat sandwich.

4 WHEN THE PIG CAME HOME

3035 Dundas St W
West End ⑥
+1 647 345 9001
whenthepig
camehome.ca

When the Pig Came Home is the place for meat lovers. The owners began selling peameal sandwiches at farmers' markets then expanded into a bricks-and-mortar store. Not only do they have great peameal, but many people rave about the *porchetta*.

5 THE MERSEYSIDE

2413 Dundas St W
West End ⑥
+1 647 679 3113
themerseyside.ca

The Merseyside is a small coffee shop that packs a lot of tasty items into such a small space. The coffee is great, and they make just about everything they serve in-store. There are only a few tables inside, so you may have to enjoy your order as a picnic.

5 great places to sample
INDIGENOUS CUISINE

---

6 **POW WOW CAFE**
   213 Augusta Avenue
   Downtown ①
   +1 416 551 7717

This tiny restaurant in the heart of Kensington Market takes traditional indigenous pow wow food and gives it a new life. The menu is small but delicious. Come to the Pow Wow Cafe to sample Ojibwe tacos. They also serve a killer brunch on Sundays filled with recipes rooted in indigenous Canadian culture.

7 **NISHDISH**
   690 Bloor St W
   Midtown ③
   +1 416 855 4085
   nishdish.com

NishDish began as a catering service and later took root in this small *marketeria*-type venue. The meals are all based on traditional Anishnabae cuisine and culture. Come here to sample items like Cedar Tea, Bison Sausage or Three Sisters' Soup, which uses the three staple foods of the Anishnabae diet; corn, beans and squash.

8 **TEA-N-BANNOCK**
   1294 Gerrard St E
   East End ⑤
   +1 416 220 2915
   teanbannock.ca

Tea-N-Bannock is a cozy place to stop by and purchase something different. Indigenous people developed a cuisine based on the seasonal offerings of mother nature and also government rations. Sample fry bread or try Trapper's Snack.

9 **RYERSON POW WOW**
AT: RYERSON UNIVERSITY
Downtown ①
ryerson.ca

This pow wow takes place in September. Held on the grounds of Ryerson University, it's easily accessible from anywhere in the city. There are all types of vendors at the pow wow that bring delicious indigenous food. Sample the food and watch some of the dancing. The location tends to vary so check the website.

10 **NA-ME-RES POW WOW**
Midtown ③
+1 416 652 0334
nameres.org/annual-traditional-pow-wow

Held during June to celebrate National Aboriginal Day as well as the summer solstice, this pow wow is a larger event hosted by the Native Men's Residence. It's a free event as well as family-friendly. Please note all indigenous events are alcohol-free. Check the current year's poster for the location.

6 POW WOW CAFE

5

HIGH-END DINING

establishments

---

11 IL COVO
585 College St
Downtown ①
+1 416 530 7585
ilcovo.ca

Il Covo is located right in the heart of Little Italy. The restaurant boasts a large selection of dishes that reflect several different regions in Italy. The portions are small, so that you can choose to sample numerous dishes.

12 LUMA
AT: TIFF BELL LIGHTBOX
350 King St W,
2nd Floor
Downtown ①
+1 647 288 4715
lumarestaurant.com

Luma is a seafood restaurant situated in the TIFF Lightbox. The large windows overlooking the street make for a great view while dining. They have a tasty seafood platter for two. Portions are small, and prices are high, but this is a great location for dinner and a show.

13 TOCA
AT: THE RITZ-CARLTON
TORONTO
181 Wellington St W
Downtown ①
+1 416 572 8008
tocarestaurant.com

Located inside the Ritz-Carlton, Toca is a very pretty establishment. Music is sometimes heard from below. The Italian-inspired food is delicious. They organize monthly wine tastings, and the weekend brunches are truly amazing. The cheese cave is a fun event that introduces participants to interesting treats like grappa-soaked cheese.

14 **ALO**

**163 Spadina Avenue,
3rd Floor
Downtown** ①
+1 416 260 2222
alorestaurant.com

Alo is a Michelin-starred restaurant. It is small and easy to miss. It's not grandiose but quiet and beautiful, and the staff is highly professional. Alo is known for its tasting menu. You can also book the chef's table, set in the kitchen for approximately 130 dollar per person.

15 **SCARAMOUCHE**

**1 Benvenuto Place
Midtown** ③
+1 416 961 8011
*scaramouche
restaurant.com*

Scaramouche is a long-established restaurant. It has found its way onto Canada's 100 Best Restaurants for several years. Their seafood dishes are particularly popular. There is both formal dining and a relaxed pasta bar. The dress code for the dining room is business casual.

12 **LUMA**

5 of the best places to pick up
POUTINE

___

16 LESLIEVILLE PUMPS

929 Queen St E
East End ⑤
+1 416 465 1313
leslievillepumps.com

Leslieville Pumps is not only about tasty poutine; it's also about a fun vibe. It's a BBQ joint, a gas station and a general store. My personal favourite is the old-style gas pump that's also a gumball machine. You can stop here on a road trip.

17 POUTINI'S

1112 Queen St W
West End ⑥
+1 647 342 3732
poutini.com

This tiny spot serves up amazing poutine. Locals go out of their way to visit. You can ask for it double layered, the pinnacle of poutine design. Poutini's has a plethora of varieties, including vegetarian. They are happy to play demo tapes if you're a member of a local band.

18 NOM NOM NOM POUTINE

707 Dundas St W
Downtown ①
+1 647 636 0707
nomnomnom.ca

Nom Nom Nom is another venue dedicated almost solely to poutine. It has a fun walk-up window with picnic tables situated on the sidewalk. For a very different style of poutine, try the Galvaude: seasoned chicken and peas, along with the traditional cheese curds and gravy.

19 KNUCKLE SANDWICH

**969 Coxwell Avenue
East York** ④
+1 647 748 7999
knucklesandwich.ca

Knuckle Sandwich isn't pretentious. This laidback spot creates freshly made sandwiches, unique versions of poutine and serves a variety of local beers. The Danforth poutine adds a Greek twist with feta cheese and capers. The patio is a comfortable place to sit on summer days. Portions are huge, so arrive hungry.

20 CLUNY BISTRO

**35 Tank House Lane
Downtown** ①
+1 416 203 2632
clunybistro.com

Cluny serves a fusion of French Canadian and classic French cuisine. The coq au vin poutine is made with chicken, red wine, bacon and cheese. It's a unique twist on this heart-stopping dish. The decor is beautiful. It sets a beautiful scene for a few Instagram photos if you're the type who likes to post your adventures.

17 POUTINI'S

5 places to sample
BUTTER TARTS

---

21 SWEET BLISS
1304 Queen St E
East End ⑤
+1 416.916.7895
sweetbliss
leslieville.com

Sweet Bliss will remind you of a rustic cottage when you walk through the door. The staff is friendly and accommodating. Everything is good here. Sample the butter tarts with a nicely crafted latte. You should also try their cinnamon buns.

22 THE MAIDS' COTTAGE
233 Main St S
Newmarket ⑪
ON L3Y 3Y9
+1 905 954 0202
themaidscottage.com

Located in the Greater Toronto Area, it's a bit of drive out of downtown to visit the Maids' Cottage. It's a good place for breakfast on your way up to the Flying Monkey Brewery as it's on the way. They have an entire counter dedicated to butter tarts.

23 DETOUR CAFE
41 King St W
Dundas ⑨
ON L9H 1T5
+1 289 238 8184
detourcoffee.com/
pages/our-cafe-detour

Detour Cafe serves beautiful artisan pastries and bread. The decor is beautiful and bright. It's a comfy spot to pick up a coffee and a sweet snack. They are primarily a coffee roaster, but the baking is on par with the quality of their coffee.

23 **DETOUR CAFE**

24 LEAH'S BAKERY

621 St Clair Avenue W
Midtown ③
+1 416 785 4711
leahs.ca

Owner Leah Kalish started baking for her own family. She established the bakery, and it quickly became a neighbourhood hotspot. Everything is made fresh daily. The butter tarts are crafted carefully, and the fresh crust is awesome. They sell their wares in a variety of different markets around town as well.

25 TORI'S BAKESHOP

2188 Queen St E
East End ⑤
+1 647 350 6500
torisbakeshop.ca

Tori's is vegan, gluten-free and organic. Many people don't realize this if they don't read the signs. Tori's stocks a delicious repertoire of baked goods. The butter tarts have a light-tasting crust with a delicious, sweet runny centre. They also make donuts and a variety of tasty sandwiches.

5 spots to find

GOURMET ICE CREAM *or* ICE-CREAM SANDWICHES

---

26 **BAKERBOTS BAKING**
205 Delaware Avenue
Midtown ③
+1 416 901 3500
bakerbotsbaking.com

Bakerbots is a tiny little bakery near Ossington that serves us huge ice-cream sandwiches. They only have one table, so expect to take your treat outside. The cookies are amazing, and they have unusual flavours of ice cream like Taro. It's a gooey treat perfect for a hot day.

27 **DUTCH DREAMS**
36 Vaughan Road
Midtown ③
+1 416 656 6959
dutchdreams.ca

Dutch Dreams is a neighbourhood staple and has been in business since 1980. They have a huge selection of flavours, and the portions are massive. If you need to share a cone, no one will tease you. The decor is quirky and fun, as well. The walls are covered in knickknacks.

28 EVA'S

454 Bloor St W
Midtown ③
+1 416 697 8884
originalchimneys.com

Eva's is another example of the diversity of Toronto. Originally from Hungary, she baked these amazing traditional chimney cakes for her family. Her grandson then worked to open the restaurant here in Toronto. This traditional cake is sweet and delicious but they've adapted the cake to create a unique cone in which they now serve some amazing soft-serve combos. My favourite is the tiramisu cone.

29 ARCTIC BITES

21 Baldwin St
Downtown ①
+1 647 247 2818
arcticbites.com

Arctic Bites' claim to fame is rolled ice cream. They pound in ingredients, spread out the ice cream and then roll it up like a sushi roll. They have lots of unique flavours – no cones here, just bowls of rolled ice cream and lots of whipped cream.

30 IHALO KRUNCH

831 Queen St W
Downtown ①
ihalokrunch.com

IHalo Krunch is the place for unique charcoal-filtered ice cream. You'll find folks wandering out of the store with weirdly coloured treats. Don't let the colours turn you off, the flavour is amazing. Just be warned: the charcoal stains your mouth black for a short period.

The 5 best places for an
AMAZING BRUNCH

31 **UNCLE BETTY'S DINER**
2590 Yonge St
Uptown ③
+1 416 483 2590
unclebettysdiner.com

Uncle Betty's is packed most weekends. Arrive early or later in the morning when the crowds thin out. Lunch is great, but brunch is the true reason to visit. This isn't a low-calorie eatery, your waistline will expand if you eat here. The vibe is laidback, and the decor is clean and simple.

32 **LADY MARMALADE**
265 Broadview Ave
East End ⑤
+1 647 351 7645
ladymarmalade.ca

Lady Marmalade is a bright and airy restaurant thanks to the many skylights on the upper level. The service is great. Lady Marmalade is best known for its eggs Benny, the hollandaise sauce is awesome. If you're not into heavy breakfasts they have lots of fruit-and vegetable-based dishes.

33 SAVING GRACE

907 Dundas St W
Downtown ①
+1 416 703 7368

Saving Grace has been in business for almost 20 years. They serve all-day breakfast, but most people arrive for brunch. There are often line-ups, so if you don't want to wait, arrive early. They have lots of unusual items on the menu, like Japanese mushrooms paired with savoury pancakes.

34 SCHOOL

70 Fraser Avenue
Downtown ②
+1 416 588 0005
schooltoronto.com

School is not a place to come when you're strapped for cash. You will not be disappointed, though. The cost reflects the quality. They don't take reservations; you have to take your chances. The decor is trendy and hip with lots of exposed brick.

35 THE STOCKYARDS SMOKEHOUSE & LARDER

699 St Clair Avenue W
Midtown ③
+1 416 658 9666
thestockyards.ca

The Stockyards is a southern-themed restaurant. Their weekday menu boasts amazing buttermilk fried chicken and their brunch is just as good. The buttermilk biscuits are soft, fresh and delicious. They do a wicked version of grilled peanut butter and banana. The space is a bit cramped, it feels like a small-town diner.

5

VEGETARIAN *or* VEGAN

restaurants

---

36 VEGANDALE BREWERY

1346 Queen St W
West End ⑥
vegandalebrewery.com

Vegandale combines the talents of a top brewer with a well-known vegan chef. The menu might remind you of a combination of McDonald's, a chicken-and-waffles joint and an American diner. The beer is very popular, and they have several varieties on tap.

37 COPENHAGEN VEGAN CAFE

1312 Queen St W
West End ⑥
+1 647 352 1312
copenhagen
vegancafe.com

Copenhagen Vegan Cafe is elegant and refined. Walking through the door feels like you've entered the past. The glass bakery shelf will have you drooling as you peruse a variety of vegan cakes and pastries. The cafe serves lunch as well as weekend brunch.

40 BLISS KITCHEN

38 PLANTA

1221 Bay St
Midtown ③
+1 647 812 1221
plantarestaurants.com

Planta is a high-end vegan restaurant. The prices, however, reflect the quality of the food. They try to source products from local producers, highlighting both ethical eating and sustainability. The dishes range from delicious sandwiches and burgers to elegant pasta dishes. They also serve biodynamic and organic wines.

39 ROSALINDA

133 Richmond St W
Downtown ①
+1 416 907 0650
rosalinda
restaurant.com

Rosalinda is a beautiful and bright modern-feeling restaurant. They serve up Mexican-inspired vegan dishes. Customers rave about the *flautas*, and the Rosa burger is very popular with those who may not be vegans but want to try the experience. They also have several tasty non-alcoholic cocktails.

40 BLISS KITCHEN

312 Dundas St E
Waterdown ⑨
ON L0R 2H0
+1 905 689 2547
blisskitchen.ca

Bliss Kitchen is more than a restaurant. They work to promote a healthy, active lifestyle. They offer a menu full of healthy vegan options and desserts. Check the website for a list of workshops you can attend, like a yoga class followed by brunch.

5 places to order a
DELICIOUS DESSERT

---

41 **SUGAR MARMALADE**
280 Spadina Avenue
Downtown ⓘ
+1 647 969 8881
sugarmarmalade.com

Try Sugar Marmalade for something a little different. This restaurant chain draws on flavours found in Hong Kong. Some of the dessert items may not sound tasty but trust me, they're awesome. Consider trying the shaved ice with strawberries.

42 **NEO COFFEE BAR**
161 Frederick St, #100
Downtown ⓘ
+1 647 348 8811
neocoffeebar.com

Neo serves up delicious organic pastries, cakes and desserts, which pair beautifully with their commitment to making great coffee. The cafe is laidback and welcoming. It's a place to come and spend time with friends or chat with strangers. They also have laptop- and cell phone-free hours on weekend afternoons.

43 **NUGATEAU**
717 Queen St W
Downtown ⓘ
+1 647 748 7001
nugateau.com

Nugateau makes eclairs. You'll find the classic eclair with cream filling and chocolate glaze, but they are especially known for their creative designs. They've created a Red Rocket eclair that pays tribute to the Toronto streetcar system.

44 THE ROLLING PIN

1970 Avenue Road
North York ⑪
+1 416 691 4554
therollingpin.ca

Sure, you can go to The Rolling Pin and order an amazing brownie, but they are the only place I know of that advertises a daily donut menu. My personal favourite is Tuesday for the Custard Bomb donut. It's amazing!

45 BALLISSIMO LOUKOUMADES BAR

1027 Coxwell Avenue
East York ④
+1 416 901 2259
ballissimo.ca

Loukoumades are the Greek version of donuts. They're light, fluffy and soaked in honey. Ballissimo serves them the traditional way, but they've taken the *loukoumades* to new heights by topping these bite-size donuts with ingredients like maple cream and pecans. They also serve fantastic specialty coffees.

43 NUGATEAU

5 restaurants in
KOREATOWN
you can visit in one night

---

46 **KOREAN VILLAGE RESTAURANT**
628 Bloor St W
Midtown ③
+1 416 536 0290
koreanvillage toronto.com

Koreatown in Toronto is basically one street, filled with awesome Korean restaurants. People will hop from place to place, picking and choosing dishes. Korean Village is one of the most popular restaurants in the area. It can be very busy, so be prepared to wait or make reservations to be safe. Pictures of the owner with celebrities line the walls. Be aware: they will challenge you if you don't tip.

47 **SUNRISE HOUSE**
661 Bloor St W
Midtown ③
+1 416 535 1019
sunrisehouse toronto.com

Sunrise House is a classic Korean restaurant that serves quick no-nonsense dishes. The tiny place is immensely popular with locals. The decor is a bit old and funky but that's not why you're visiting, you're here to sample spicy delicious food. I visit every year when I need my fix of the seafood pancake. It's truly incredible.

48 BARRIO COREANO

642 Bloor St W
Midtown ③
+1 416 901 5188
playacabana.ca/barrio

Barrio Coreano combines Mexican with Korean flavours. The restaurant has a lovely, comfortable atmosphere, and the unique combination of cultural influences makes for some interesting dishes. For example, they make a delicious chipotle-sesame salsa.

49 LIM GA NE KOREAN RESTAURANT

686 Bloor St W
Midtown ③
+1 647 435 2700

It's easy to find Lim Ga Ne, just look for the large bright orange sign out front. The restaurant is small and homey. It's open late, and the portions are huge. They serve a lot of dishes you won't find in other Korean restaurants. Be brave! Try some unusual dishes. It's best to just show up at Lim Ga Ne, they don't always answer the phone and if they do, they might answer in Korean.

50 TACOS EL ASADOR

689 Bloor St W
Midtown ③
+1 416 538 9747

El Asador is a family-run restaurant with history. The small venue has been a part of Koreatown for almost 20 years. The family arrived here from El Salvador during the country's civil war. Over the years, they've built up the restaurant, which delights hungry visitors with authentic Mexican and Salvadorean cuisine.

5 restaurants where you can find
FIERY JERK CHICKEN

---

51 RASTA PASTA

61 Kensington Ave
Downtown ①
+1 647 501 4505
eatrastapasta.ca

The name Rasta Pasta reflects the true nature of this establishment. They combine Jamaican with Italian cuisine. You can try dishes like shrimp curry linguine or jerk lasagna; if you're not into fusion dishes, they offer a tasty authentic jerk chicken with just the right amount of spice.

52 FAHMEE BAKERY & JAMAICAN FOODS

119 Montezuma Trail
Scarborough ⑦
ON M1V 1J4
+1 416 754 2126
fahmeebakery.com

Fahmee is located in Scarborough. The bakery decor is a little run-down, like most of Scarborough. Don't let the area colour your opinion, Fahmee is delicious. The coco bread with jerk pork is a fantastic filling choice. This is Jamaican food at its best. Spicy, fresh and simply good.

53 MR. JERK

209 Wellesley St E
Downtown ①
+1 416 961 8913
mrjerktoronto.ca

There are several locations of Mr. Jerk around the GTA (Greater Toronto Area). The chain has become pretty popular. It's a great place to eat in, take out or get jerk delivered to your doorstep. Like most Jamaican restaurants, it's not about the dining experience, but about having quick, cheap, delicious food.

54 CHRIS JERK

2570 Birchmount Rd
Scarborough ⑦
ON M1T 2M5
+1 416 297 5375

Chris Jerk fuses Middle Eastern with Jamaican cooking. The most popular items are jerk shawarma and jerk chicken poutine. There's always a line-up at lunchtime. Arrive after the rush to pick up your takeout. There isn't much else around, so consider taking your lunch to a park across the 404.

55 ALLWYN'S BAKERY

976 The Queensway
Etobicoke ⑧
ON M8Z 1P6
+1 647 351 0688

Allwyn's Bakery has expanded from humble roots to several locations throughout the GTA. They plan to add another location on the University of Toronto Campus. They are open well past midnight for those who need a late-night snack. Jerk chicken with rice and peas is the perfect combination.

5 ITALIAN RESTAURANTS

that serve more than pasta

---

56 PIZZERIA LIBRETTO
550 Danffforth Avenue
East End ⑤
+1 416 466 0400
pizzerialibretto.com

Pizzeria Libretto is a small eatery with a laidback vibe. It's always packed on the weekends, but you can usually find space at the bar to sip cocktails, chat with the bartender and dine. Try the *burrata* with *prosciutto di parma*, tomatoes and herbs.

57 ANNETTE FOOD MARKET
240 Annette St
West End ⑥
+1 416 519 4103
annettefood market.com

Annette Food Market has amazing wood-fired pizzas you can pair with a vast selection of wine by the glass or bottle. The food is fresh and delicious. Located off of Dundas, it's not a large restaurant and easily missed if you're not a local. Make a reservation to ensure you get a table.

58 ARDO RESTAURANT
243 King St E
Downtown ①
+1 647 347 8930
ardorestaurant.com

Ardo is a Sicilian-inspired Italian bistro-style restaurant. The food here is much more authentic than the dishes you usually find in typical Italian restaurants. Ingredients are fresh, and the colours are bright. Many of the pasta dishes are completely house-made.

59 BAR BUCA
75 Portland St
Downtown ①
+1 416 599 2822
buca.ca/bar.html

Bar Buca is a trendy cafe spot located in King West that changes their menu seasonally. They try their best to source local and sustainable ingredients. Open at 7.30 am, you can visit for breakfast, lunch or dinner. They also serve brunch on the weekends.

60 ENOTECA SOCIALE
1288 Dundas St W
West End ⑥
+1 416 534 1200
sociale.ca

Enoteca Sociale prides itself on being a wine bar with great food. They make fantastic gnocchi and have many wines to pair with this dish. The menu is smaller but covers all realms of Italian food, from salads to pasta and *secondi*. They have a nice patio, if somewhat cramped.

57 ANNETTE FOOD MARKET

5 restaurants that feature
FLAVOURS FROM AROUND THE WORLD

---

61 GLORY OF INDIA ROTI CUISINE

1407 Queen St W
West End ⑥
+1 647 349 5679
gloryofindiaonline.ca

Glory of India is a very small mom-and-pop joint in Parkdale. Most people order takeout. It's a no-nonsense restaurant where the food is good and the service is quick. The interior is simple and clean, with bright windows. All the dishes are tasty, but most locals love the Chicken Vindaloo.

62 SI LOM

534 Church St
Downtown ①
+1 416 515 0888
silom.ca

Si Lom is a quiet, unassuming Thai restaurant located in the heart of the gay village. The food is very authentic. Portions are sizeable and reasonably priced. A personal favourite is the soft-shell crab. There's a comfy modern vibe that pervades this restaurant. You'll be pleasantly surprised when you arrive.

63 BAMIYAN KABOB

62 Overlea Blvd,
Unit 3A
East York ④
+1 416 429 7514
bamiyankabob.com

You can find Bamiyan Kabob stores all over the GTA. The restaurant began as one small Afghan venue, and the popularity of the food grew quickly. Bamiyan is primarily a takeout joint. The Kofta Kabob is very yummy. They've taken Afghan food and made it accessible to North American palettes.

64 TO-NE SUSHI

414 Queen St W
Downtown ①
+1 416 866 8200
tonesushi.com

The best description of To-Ne is to say it's a small restaurant that makes really pretty sushi. Their presentation is beautiful. The other bonus to To-Ne is that they don't overfill the sushi with large amounts of rice; the ingredient-to-rice ratio is perfect. Reservation is recommended on weekend evenings.

65 EMERALD CHINESE RESTAURANT

30 Eglinton Ave W
Mississauga ⑧
ON L5R 3E7
+1 905 890 9338
*emeraldchinese
restaurant.com*

Located close to Square One Shopping Centre, Emerald looks like any other Chinese restaurant. But don't let appearances fool you. They have one thing on the menu that definitely sets them apart from the rest: their dim sum. The huge selection of steamed buns they serve is as authentic as it is delicious.

The 5 best places to get
AWESOME BURGERS

---

66 BOON BURGER CAFE OAKVILLE

497 Dundas St W
Oakville ⑨
ON L6M 4M2
+1 905 257 0799
boonburger.ca

Boon Burger's line of vegan burgers is popular with both meat lovers and veggie lovers. They serve up classic burger flavours with a vegan twist. Order a side of chili cheese fries and a glass of wine with your burger. Boon Burger also serves vegan pizza and soft serve.

67 WOODY'S BURGERS

3795 Lake Shore
Boulevard W
Etobicoke ⑧
ON M8W 1R2
+1 416 546 2093
woodysburgers.ca

Woody's prides themselves on serving handmade burgers topped with as many local ingredients as they can find. They proudly advertise their connection to local beef operations. Like most burger joints, their dishes are served in baskets lined with wax paper. Burgers are huge. You will leave completely stuffed.

68 HOLY CHUCK

1450 Yonge St
Downtown ①
+1 416 962 4825
holychuckburgers.com

Holy Chuck looks like any other fast-food restaurant, and some of the burgers will remind you of some large fast-food chains. But they also serve up a six-patty burger, as well as a burger with different types of meat patties. Don't forget a milkshake; they're amazing.

69 THE SKYLINE RESTAURANT

1426 Queen St W
West End ⑥
+1 416 536 3682

The Skyline is a neighbourhood diner. It's cozy; the decor hasn't changed since its original opening, and the vibe is welcoming. Their menu is pretty standard, they serve up classic greasy diner burgers. The difference is that they use really good quality ingredients, which turns typical diner food into something special.

70 THE CARBON BAR

99 Queen St E
Downtown ①
+1 416 947 7000
thecarbonbar.ca

The Carbon Bar is a dark, lively establishment with a large menu offering anything from ribs to seafood, salads and burgers. They do meat properly. The burger comes on an artisan bun, and the patty is juicy and filling. Some dishes may be average, but their unassuming burger is a highlight.

5

PUBS

with great food

---

71 **THE STONE LION**
   1958 Queen St E
   East End ⑤
   +1 416 690 1984
   stonelionpub.com

The Stone Lion is a popular neighbourhood pub located in the Beaches. It has a nice patio, and the fare is simple, standard pub food. It is quite tasty however, and you won't be disappointed with the chicken wings or the crispy cauliflower.

72 **ALLEN'S**
   143 Danforth Avenue
   East End ⑤
   +1 416 463 3086
   allens.to

Allen's is a little fancier than the average pub. The back patio is lovely; there's a huge willow that drapes down over the diners. Allen's has an extensive menu, including some awesome burgers. It's the type of spot where you will feel right at home.

73 **THE QUEEN AND BEAVER PUBLIC HOUSE**
   35 Elm St
   Downtown ①
   +1 647 347 2712
   queenandbeaverpub.ca

It doesn't get much more British than The Queen and Beaver. The menu here is more British than in most of the pubs you'll find in the UK. They even do Sunday Roast. Not many pubs are dedicated to creating such an authentic Victorian vibe. It's a pretty building, great for Instagram photos.

74 BRYDEN'S

2455 Bloor St W
West End ⑥
+1 416 760 8069
brydens.ca

Bryden's is a quiet pub serving some of the best food around. It's nothing flashy, but the nachos are well worth the visit, loaded with tasty fresh toppings. The patio is small, sunny and comfortable. The walls are lined with an eclectic array of decor.

75 PETER PAN BISTRO

373 Queen St W
Downtown ①
+1 416 792 3838
peterpanbistro.ca

The Peter Pan Bistro is a lovely, dark pub filled with ambiance and centrally located in Toronto. They host regular wine-coaching nights. Pay a fee and learn about a variety of wines from one of their experts. Try Tuesday night steak night or order a salad at lunchtime.

73 THE QUEEN AND BEAVER PUBLIC HOUSE

5

FOOD FESTIVALS

not to miss

---

76 **TASTE OF THE DANFORTH**
Danforth Avenue
East End ⑤
tasteofthedanforth.com

Taste of the Danforth is a staple festival in Toronto. Wander along Danforth Avenue, sampling a variety of dishes. Located in Greektown, you can make a guess at the main theme. It's also a great time to meet professional sports players. Many of the Raptors and Maple Leafs will make guest appearances.

77 **THE MAC AND CHEESE FESTIVAL**
AT: ROUNDHOUSE PARK
255 Bremner Blvd
Downtown ②
themacandcheese
festival.com

The Mac and Cheese Festival is a terrible place to visit on a diet. Vendors serve up versions of this North American staple. Chefs are challenged to be creative and come up with their interpretations of this simple dish. Past experiments have included Nacho or Lobster Mac and Cheese.

78 MOMO CRAWL T.O.

Queen St W between O'Hara and Dowling West End ⑥

parkdalevillagebia.com/tag/momo-crawl

Momos are delicious steamed Nepali and Tibetan dumplings. These bite-size treats come in both vegetarian and meat options with a variety of spices and sauces. A pass is just 25 dollar. It's a small festival that lets you wander through the Parkdale neighbourhood at the same time.

79 JERKFEST TORONTO

AT: CENTENNIAL PARK

256 Centennial Park Road

Etobicoke ⑧

ON M9C 5N3

jerkfestival.ca

JerkFest is a family-friendly festival with an impressive lineup of R&B and reggae performers. Consider purchasing tickets for the gala event aboard the double-decker boat, the River Gambler. Make sure you try the Escovitch Salmon and the Jerk Chicken.

80 TORONTO VEGANDALE FOOD AND DRINK FESTIVAL

AT: GARRISON COMMON – FORT YORK

250 Fort York Blvd Downtown ②

vegandalefest.com/toronto

Visiting Fort York during the Vegandale Food Festival is a great way to see one of Toronto's historic sites while getting to experience the variety of cuisine available in this multicultural city. Take in the fort's history, then stop to sample delicious vegan recipes from local vendors.

The 5 best **BANH MI RESTAURANTS**

around Toronto

---

81 BANH MI NGUYEN HUONG

322 Spadina Avenue
Downtown ①
+1 416 599 4625
nguyenhuong.ca

Locals who love Nguyen Huong are intensely loyal. They've been visiting for years. The counter here is huge and acts as an assembly line of baguettes and toppings. The bread is lovely and fresh. Take your *bahn mi* to go and find a lovely park bench to enjoy your meal.

82 ROSE'S VIETNAMESE SANDWICHES

601 Gerrard St E
East End ⑤
+1 416 406 9906

Rose's isn't fancy. It embodies the old Chinatown sensibilities. Their *banh mi* is tasty, simple and cheap. The takeout counter provides lots of options and loads of pickled radish. Just don't expect the folks behind the counter to cater to your whims.

83 BAGUETTE & CO.

2772 Dundas St W
West End ⑥
+1 647 344 1933
baguetteco.ca

This is the first establishment on the list that is not solely dedicated to *banh mi*. Baguette & Co. focuses on serving sandwiches and salads. Since baguettes are so important in *banh mi,* the quality of their bread makes this sandwich amazing.

84 SNACK SHACK

**3260 Lake Shore
Boulevard W
Etobicoke ⑧
ON M8V 1M4
+1 647 508 5777**

The Snack Shack is an unexpected find with an eclectic menu. You'll find a strange mix of items on the menu. Everything is good, but many come here just for the *banh mi*. You won't get an authentic *banh mi* experience, but you will pick up a good sandwich.

85 RUSTLE & STILL

**605 Bloor St W
Midtown ③
+1 647 350 8893
*rustleandstill.com***

Rustle & Still is a cafe with Vietnamese owners who bring the very best of Vietnamese hospitality to their establishment. They serve Vietnamese coffee and *banh mi*, along with other traditional Vietnamese eats. The decor is bright and airy. The Hojicha Lattes are also awesome.

85 RUSTLE & STILL

AMSTERDAM BREWHOUSE

65 PLACES TO GO FOR A DRINK

---

5 bars with
GREAT FOOD

---

86 416 SNACK BAR
181 Bathurst St
Downtown ①
+1 416 364 9320
416snackbar.com/menu

This is very much a hipster bar with a cozy vibe. You won't find any meals here. You're meant to come to pick up a drink, get comfy and enjoy a snack. The menu changes regularly, and you'll never be able to pin them down to any type of specific cuisine.

87 GRAND ELECTRIC
1330 Queen St W
West End ⑥
+1 416 627 3459
*grandelectric
toronto.com/parkdale*

The best description for the food at Grand Electric is reinvented Mexican. Settle down and sample their tuna ceviche, spicy squid and a margarita. This bar is loud and lively. They play old-school hip-hop while diners enjoy a great night of good drinks and food.

88 THE PORCH

250 Adelaide St W
Downtown ①
+1 647 344 1234
theporchto.com

The Porch has great food and drinks, but one of the best things about this spot is the view from its rooftop patio. They also offer some fun events. Check the website, and you might be able to participate in a Mimosa and Yoga rooftop session. Since The Porch is an outdoor space, it is subject to Canadian weather. It will be open late spring through to early fall. You can find their closing dates online.

89 ALLEYCATZ RESTAURANT LOUNGE

2409 Yonge St
Uptown ③
+1 416 481 6865
alleycatz.ca

Alleycatz has a unique vibe. It's a supper club and bar. They have several preset dinner menus. The items should best be described as Mediterranean fusion. After dinner they clear away the tables to make room for dancing and couples fill the dance floor.

90 PRETTYUGLY BAR

1237 Queen St W
West End ⑥
prettyuglybar.com

PrettyUgly is pretty impressive. The four-tiered bar is beautiful. It makes for lovely pictures. The food is provided by Vit Beo, a local Vietnamese restaurant. It is amazing. Try pairing the dumplings with a cocktail.

5
CRAFT BREWERIES
creating awesome suds

---

91 **LEFT FIELD BREWERY**
36 Wagstaff Drive
East End ⑤
+1 647 346 5001
leftfieldbrewery.ca

You can find Left Field beers in lots of establishments throughout the GTA. A visit to the actual brewery is a lot more fun, though. The highlight of this brewery is joining them in the taproom for a beer and a Jay's game. They show every game for the loyal fans.

92 **BLOOD BROTHERS BREWING**
165 Geary Avenue
Midtown ③
+1 647 628 6062
bloodbrothers brewing.com

Blood Brothers serves a wide variety of uniquely flavoured brews. Loyal customers will insist their favourite is the best. The taproom doesn't serve food. It's more about picking up some beer and enjoying a drink on site.

93 **AMSTERDAM BREWHOUSE**
245 Queens Quay W
Downtown ②
+1 416 504 1020
amsterdambeer.com/ brewhouse

The Amsterdam BrewHouse has several locations in Toronto. Book a tour for a Saturday morning and then enjoy lunch at the Leaside location. The brewhouse on the Queens Quay is more of a restaurant offering their beer. Order a flight of beers and wood-fired pizza; it's a great combo.

94 **CAMERON'S BREWING**
1165 Invicta Drive
Oakville ⑨
ON L6H 4M1
+1 905 849 8282
cameronsbrewing.com

Cameron's is a no-nonsense brewery that prides themselves on sourcing high-quality ingredients. You can book a tour of the brewery, and then purchase some different lagers to take with you for an evening picnic. The growlers are a particularly fun purchase.

95 **FLYING MONKEYS CRAFT BREWERY**
107 Dunlop St E
Barrie ⑪
ON L4M 1A6
+1 705 806 7089
flyingmonkeys.ca

Barrie is approximately 45 minutes north of Toronto, but it's worth visiting the area and taking a tour of Flying Monkeys. They offer a variety of different brews, and one of the highlights of this brand is the bright and colourful collectable designs on the cans.

The 5 best patios where you can
ENJOY A SUMMER EVENING

---

96 BAR NEON
1226 Bloor St W
West End ⑥
+1 647 748 6366
barneon.ca

Bar Neon boasts a beautiful back patio complete with strings of lights and picnic tables. Small and intimate, this is a great place to sample a craft brew. Perhaps you prefer a cocktail? They've got some great ones. The Greek salad is amazing. The owner takes pride in serving dishes that reflect her heritage.

97 THE WAVY WALL CRAFT KITCHEN
AT: GREAT LAKES BREWERY
30 Queen Elizabeth Boulevard
Etobicoke ⑨
ON M8Z 1LB
+1 800 463 5435
greatlakesbeer.com/ wavy-wall

The Wavy Wall Craft Kitchen is kid- and pet-friendly, with a laidback patio. You can enjoy a reasonably priced entrée and one of their craft beers. It's easy to access, right off the highway and only a short trip from downtown. The beer names often reflect elements of Toronto.

98 BETTY'S

240 King St E
Downtown ①
+1 416 368 1300
bettysonking.com

Betty's has been around for a long time. It's a well-established dive bar in the St. Lawrence district. The beautiful patio is surrounded by honey locust trees. It can get pretty packed and wild on weekends, so be prepared for a loud evening of fun.

99 SKY YARD

AT: THE DRAKE HOTEL
1150 Queen St W
West End ⑥
+1 416 531 5042
thedrake.ca

The Drake Hotel is just one of those places you have to visit. It has been a part of Toronto for a long time, and everyone knows The Drake. The Sky Yard won't disappoint; it's trendy with lots of ambience, but also very busy. Arrive early to get a table.

100 MILL STREET BREW PUB

21 Tank House Lane
Downtown ①
+1 416 681 0338
millstreetbrewery.com

Mill Street may not be a hidden secret to locals. The place is packed with people on their lunch break or enjoying dinner still in their office wear. The patio is huge. It's filled with comfy seating, from which you can enjoy a Mill Street brew paired with brunch. Try the pierogis and eggs.

5
COFFEE BARS
with comfy seating

---

101 CAFE NEON

**241 Wallace Avenue
West End** ⑥
+1 647 352 8366
cafeneon.ca

Cafe Neon is the sister establishment to Bar Neon. The owner styled the cafe after the Greek *kafenio's* (coffee houses). The vibe is comfortable and laidback. The excellent coffee is sourced from a local vendor, and the baked goods are made daily in-house. Enjoy the all-day breakfast.

102 **DINEEN COFFEE CO.**

102 DINEEN COFFEE CO.

140 Yonge St
Downtown ①
+1 416 900 0949
dineencoffee.com

Dineen Coffee is located in a Toronto heritage building. It used to be a fur clothing factory. The interior is pretty and bright with large wrap-around windows that let you watch life pass by. I like the large wooden coffee bar. They have a very nice patio out front.

103 SNAKES AND LATTES ANNEX

600 Bloor St W
Midtown ③
+1 647 342 9229
snakesandlattes.com/
location/annex

Everyone loves Snakes and Lattes. You can't go wrong when you visit with friends. Not only do they serve up great coffee in a comfy setting, but you can also spend a rainy afternoon here comfortably playing a variety of board games. It's a lot of fun here.

104 WHITE SQUIRREL

907 Queen St W
Downtown ①
+1 647 428 4478
whitesquirrel
coffee.com

White Squirrel serves fair trade organic coffee and tea, along with a variety of sandwiches. They also serve Greg's Ice Cream, which is made locally. The map of Toronto that fills an entire wall can be quite useful for those trying to establish a sense of direction.

105 OUT OF THIS WORLD CAFE

100 Stokes St
Downtown ①
+1 416 535 8501
ext.33006
otwcafe.com

Out of this World is the cafe run by CAMH, a well-respected mental health institution in Toronto. A visit and a purchase from the cafe helps to support the continued work of CAMH. The institution helps so many Torontonians in need of assistance.

5 amazing
NIGHTCLUBS
to dance the night away

---

106 PARLOUR
270 Adelaide St W
Downtown ①
+1 416 408 3666
parlour270.com

Stepping into Parlour feels like, well, stepping into a Victorian parlour. There are red velvet curtains and elegant seating everywhere. This isn't a large venue, and you will most likely have to wait in line. There is also a dress code, so don't show up in ripped jeans.

107 LOST AND FOUND
577 King St W
Downtown ①
+1 647 995 5772
lost577.com

Lost and Found can best be described as a new club trying to attract all the hottest and hippest folks in Toronto. The bar features a lot of local hip-hop artists. Many people come for the music. The bouncers can be quite picky about who they allow inside.

108 NEST
423 College St
Downtown ①
+1 416 792 9488
nest.to

Nest is located on the second floor of a large building. If you've been drinking, the stairs can be a challenge. The cover charge is reasonable. This is the place to go if you like to dance the night away. Nest hosts both local DJs as well as international guests.

109 REBEL

11 Polson St
Downtown ②
rebelpolson.com

Rebel is truly all about live music. It features an impressive line-up of local performers as well as travelling acts. The venue is huge. Most of the music falls into the category of alternative. Locals may still know the venue by its former name, Sound Academy.

110 CODA

794 Bathurst St
Midtown ③
+1 416 536 0346
codatoronto.com

Coda has a large dance floor and several small bar areas that make getting drinks and dancing easy. The sound system is excellent here, and the music is always conducive to dancing. The price of drinks is fairly average. Coda is a much less pretentious club than others in Toronto.

108 **NEST**

5 small venues for
LIVE MUSIC

___

111 GLADSTONE HOTEL

1214 Queen St W
West End ⑥
+1 416 531 4635
gladstonehotel.com

The Gladstone is a historic building in Toronto. The venue has a small pub and stage on the main floor. This is the place to find great cover bands and enjoy a quality meal. There's also karaoke on Saturday nights. Upstairs you'll find hotel rooms you can book for the night. It's a popular place so book well in advance.

112 C'EST WHAT

67 Front St E
Downtown ①
+1 416 867 9499
cestwhat.com

It's easy to miss this bar. The signage is small, and you need to head down a large flight of stairs to the basement. It opens up to a dining area on one side, and a pub on the other. Live bands take over on Friday and Saturday nights.

113 BOVINE SEX CLUB

542 Queen St W
Downtown ①
+1 416 504 4239
bovinesexclub.com

The Bovine Sex Club is a must if you are into alternative music. It has been a staple in Toronto for years. This edgy dive bar is not the place to spend a quiet, relaxed evening. It's gritty, yet vibrant. The Tiki patio bar is amazing.

114 THE DAKOTA TAVERN

249 Ossington Ave
Downtown ①
+1 416 850 4579
thedakotatavern.com

The Dakota Tavern has a unique Sunday brunch. For a 5 dollar cover at the door, you can enjoy bluegrass bands and purchase a tasty brunch meal. They serve a delicious cocktail called the Breakfast Mule: it's a combo of vodka, ginger beer and grapefruit juice.

115 THE GARRISON

1197 Dundas St W
Downtown ①
+1 416 519 9439
garrisontoronto.com

The Garrison is small, dark and gritty. There's a small stage, and table space is limited, but they feature an impressive line-up of up-and-coming bands. They play the music loud, so if you're sensitive bring earplugs or purchase a pair from the bar.

111 GLADSTONE HOTEL

The 5 swankiest places to find
HIGH-END COCKTAILS

---

116 LOBBY LOUNGE
AT: SHANGRI-LA HOTEL
188 University Ave
Downtown ①
+1 647 788 8281
shangri-la.com

The Lobby Lounge is located in the lobby of the Shangri-La Hotel. It's about as swanky as you can get in Toronto. It's beautiful, filled with natural light and comfy seating. The cocktails are mixed with care. You can enjoy the view of the unique sculpture that graces the entrance.

117 BAR RAVAL
505 College St
Downtown ①
+1 647 344 8001
thisisbarraval.com

Even if you're not a drinker, visiting Bar Raval for the decor is a worthy endeavour. The bar is beautifully designed using African mahogany. The cocktails are excellent; my personal favourite is Into the Sun. The Fried Eggplant & Honey tapas is the best dish on the menu.

118 CIVIL LIBERTIES
878 Bloor St W
Midtown ③
+1 416 546 5634
civillibertiesbar.com

Civil Liberties operates on a unique principle: there is no set cocktail list. Instead, bartenders will mix up unique cocktails based on the whims of patrons. They have a small menu of bar snacks, or you can order from Vit Beo, the Vietnamese restaurant next door.

119 PRAVDA VODKA
44 Wellington St E
Downtown ①
+1 416 366 0303
pravdavodkabar.com

It's not cheap to visit Pravda; there is a minimum table charge when booking a private spot. They do have an amazing variety of vodkas and cocktails. It's fun to chat with the server about which vodka to pair with different plates of food.

120 COLD TEA
60 Kensington Ave
Downtown ①
+1 416 546 4536

Located in Kensington Mall, it seems an odd spot to find some nicely made cocktails. Cold Tea has an Asian-inspired menu. It's not easy to find; the entranceway is marked by a red light. Listen for the sound of the music rather than looking for a sign.

116 LOBBY LOUNGE

5

CANADIAN WINERIES

a short drive from the city

---

121 **WESTCOTT VINEYARDS**

3180 Seventeenth St
Jordan ⑩
ON LoR 1So
+1 905 562 7517
westcottvineyards.com

Westcott is a small family-run vineyard. The highlight of this establishment is the tasting room and the wood-burning fireplace. During the winter and fall, book for 'Fireside Fridays', when visiting chefs prepare special menus that pair with their wines. It's an intimate and very unique dining experience.

121 WESTCOTT VINEYARDS

122 RED STONE WINES

4245 King St
Beamsville ⑩
ON LoR 1B1
+1 905 563 9463
redstonewines.ca

Red Stone is an organic and biodynamic winery. The winery is owned by bigwig Moray Tawse. He brings an impressive knowledge of wine to Red Stone. They also host weekly summer concerts and offer an impressive menu in their restaurant.

123 SUE-ANN STAFF ESTATE WINERY

3210 Staff Avenue
Jordan ⑩
ON LoR 1So
+1 905 562 1719
sue-annstaff.com

Sue-Ann Staff is a small family-owned winery. Sue-Ann primarily grows Riesling grapes on the property. A visit to her tasting room, located in the kitchen, is a unique and intimate experience. Sue-Ann Staff is known as the queen of ice wine, so make sure to try it when you visit.

124 ADAMO ESTATE WINERY

793366 3rd Line EHS
Mono ⑪
ON L9W 5X7
+1 519 942 3969
ext.5100
adamoestate.com

Adamo Estate is off the wine trail. It's a true hidden gem located in the Dufferin Highlands. The microclimate in this part of Ontario requires Adamo to select cold weather grapes. The food is excellent, and the view from the property is fantastic. Consider this a boutique winery.

125 TEACHING WINERY

AT: NIAGARA COLLEGE
135 Taylor Road
Niagara-on-the-Lake ⑩
ON LoS 1Jo
niagaracollegewine.ca

This is a unique experience that is loads of fun. The college winery isn't flashy. You can sample wines created as final thesis projects for up-and-coming graduates. There are opportunities to chat with students and learn more about winemaking. The college also has a brewery and new distillery.

5 places that serve
UNIQUE CAESARS

---

126 TABULE

2901 Bayview Avenue
North York ⑪
+1 416 222 5424
tabulebayview.com

Tabule is another popular site that began with one restaurant and now owns several locations in the GTA. They've concocted a delicious version of a Caesar cocktail. Instead of the usual rim spice, they've used za'atar seasoning and Kaffir lime to flavour this Canadian classic.

CAESAR COCKTAIL

127 RODNEY'S OYSTER HOUSE

469 King St W
Downtown ①
+1 416 363 8105
rodneysoyster
house.com

A Caesar always pairs well with seafood. Rodney's Oyster House knows it well. They've used Walter's *(waltercaesar.com)* mix for their house blend. For a garnish, they've added a large fresh gulf shrimp. It's spicy and acidic, just the way a Caesar is supposed to taste.

128 CHERRY STREET BAR-B-QUE

275 Cherry St
Downtown ②
+1 416 461 5111
cherrystbbq.com

Cherry Street Bar-B-Que is a no-frills joint focused on southern-style BBQ. That's why it seems funny they'd create such a tasty version of this Canadian cocktail. They serve their Caesar flavoured with BBQ sauce, tamarind sauce and a whole rib as a garnish.

129 HUNTERS LANDING

82 Fort York Blvd
Downtown ②
+1 647 352 6082
hunterslanding.ca

Ordering a Hunters Landing Caesar is pretty much ordering a meal and a cocktail in one. Their version comes garnished with everything but the kitchen sink. You'll need to munch on all the garnishes before you can get to this version, which is full of real horseradish.

130 FARMHOUSE TAVERN

1627 Dupont St
West End ⑥
+1 416 561 9114

FARMHOUSE Tavern is a cozy restaurant that serves up a great brunch on Sunday, followed by an hourly special on their Caesars. They are garnished with lots of different ingredients. Much of the menu depends on what's available locally, and you will find it's different almost every week.

5 laidback spots to experience
LGBT2Q CULTURE

131 BUDDIES IN BAD TIMES THEATRE

12 Alexander St
Downtown ①
+1 416 975 8555
buddiesin
badtimes.com

Buddies in Bad Times is a local theatre company that also doubles as a nightclub and bar. Established almost 40 years ago, Buddies is the longest-running queer theatre in the world. It gives local artists and actors a place where they can celebrate diversity.

132 CREWS AND TANGOS

508 Church St
Downtown ①
+1 647 349 7469
crewsandtangos.com

It's hard to miss Crews and Tangos. The rainbow painted on the nearby crosswalk lets you know you're in the Gay Village. The exterior of Crews and Tangos is just as vibrant. They feature drag shows several nights a week on a small stage. It's a fun and intimate bar that's a little on the basic side.

133 O'GRADY'S ON CHURCH

518 Church St
Downtown ①
+1 416 323 2822
ogradyschurch.com

O'Grady's serves the typical pub fare, accompanied by the usual cocktails and beers. You won't find exotic items on the menu, but the food is delicious. O'Grady's offers something more: they organize fun activities every night of the week. Their bingo night is hilarious and loads of fun for all.

134 **THE BEAVER**

1192 Queen St W
West End ⑥
+1 416 537 2768
thebeavertoronto.com

The Beaver is a fun late-night bar and karaoke joint that organizes drag nights. The menu is basic but delicious, and cocktails are reasonably priced at around 9 dollar each. It's best to bring cash; they don't accept debit cards and there is a minimum charge on credit cards.

135 **STRIKER SPORTS BAR**

31 Saint Joseph St
Downtown ①
+1 416 929 9595
strikertoronto.ca

On the surface, Striker appears to be just like every other sports bar, with large TVs and lots of beer, but it's situated in the heart of the gay village. If it's sports-related, they will happily put it on display. They actively promote gay sports alongside Major League Baseball games.

132 RAINBOW CORNER NEAR CREWS AND TANGOS

The 5 perfect bars for
WATCHING THE GAME

---

136 TALLBOYS
838 Bloor St W
Midtown ③
+1 416 535 7486
tallboyscraft.com

Tallboys are about beer and sports. They've got two large TVs and a projection screen. They are also committed to serving only Ontario craft beers. There's a large garage door that opens up onto the street. You can watch a game and support Ontario craft beer businesses at the same time.

137 THE AVIARY
484 A Front St E
Downtown ①
+1 647 352 7837
aviarybrewpub.com

The Aviary is a fun and comfortable pub with lots of big screens and some comfy couches that are perfect for watching the game. They serve tasty vegetarian as well as meat burgers. The decor is fun, with lots of bright yellow accents.

138 THE BALLROOM
145 John St
Downtown ①
+1 416 597 2695
theballroom.ca

The Ballroom has it all. Come here to watch a game or play a few games yourself. They've got bowling and lots of pool tables. The pub offers a VIP booth and bottle service. They also do a lot of large corporate events, so be aware if you come without reservations.

139 THE DOCK ELLIS

1280 Dundas St W
West End ⑥
+1 416 792 8472
thedockellis.com

The Dock Ellis is a classic darkly lit sports bar with a modern twist. They have an awesome selection of typical bar foods like nachos and chicken wings. A multitude of TVs hang above the bar. They've also got shuffleboard and foosball tables for those who get restless.

140 ROUND THE HORN

331 Roncesvalles Ave
West End ⑥
+1 416 785 2123

Round the Horn is a true neighbourhood bar. There's a large bar to belly up to while snacking on free candy. TVs are always broadcasting the latest sports event. The food is solid, and there's a hotdog menu available until 2 am.

138 THE BALLROOM

5 bars where it's ok to
BRING YOUR OWN FOOD

---

141 WATSON'S

388 Richmond St W, #2A
Downtown ①
+1 647 347 7374
watsonstoronto.com

Watson's would best be described as super fun. There are lots of great takeout places right near here, so choose your favourite, then head into Watson's for a craft brew or a cocktail. They've also got a ton of board games that will help you pass the time.

142 THIRSTY AND MISERABLE

197 Baldwin St
Downtown ①
+1 647 607 0134

This is a dive bar that doesn't pretend to be anything else. It's small and cramped, and the beer list written on scrap cardboard is always changing. They are cash only, and they don't serve wine or cocktails. There are lots of craft beers available.

143 TRANZAC CLUB

292 Brunswick Ave
Downtown ①
+1 416 923 8137
tranzac.org

Tranzac is the oddball on this list. It's a community-run location that turns into a bar on weekends. The local Toronto rugby club, The Nomads, uses the Tranzac Club for social events. You can bring food here and enjoy their open stage nights.

144 WIDE OPEN

139a Spadina Ave
Downtown ①
+1 416 727 5411
wideopenbar.ca

Wide Open is known for its cheap drinks. People flock here to get reasonably priced drinks and enjoy the dark bare-bones interior. It's small and cramped with lots of very dark areas around the tables. They have a good selection of beers, and they make a decent mixed drink.

145 LUCKY SHRIKE

850 Dundas St W
Downtown ①
+1 416 815 7777

Lucky Shrike is a little more upscale than some of the other dive bars on this list. The patio is awesome. It's surrounded by some pretty fencing and lit with Christmas lights. The greenery makes the space quite comfortable. They make an excellent Mai Tai cocktail.

141 WATSON'S

5

SHISHA BARS

that may or may not serve alcohol

---

146 SHISHA LICIOUS

803 Dundas St E
Mississauga ⑧
ON L4Y 2B7
+1 905 232 0105
shishaliciouscafe.ca

Shisha Licious is a dark, comfortable shisha bar that serves food and has lots of different flavours of shisha. All pipes come with removable plastic mouthpieces so you can share them with friends. The decor is Middle Eastern-themed, with lots of tables but also comfy couches to relax in.

147 MANDALA

10670 Yonge St
Richmond Hill ⑪
ON L4C 3C9
+1 905 237 7969
mandalacafe.ca

Mandala recently underwent renovations, and the result is a very refined space that is well ventilated. The decor is modern, and the servers are very helpful. There are lots of varieties of shisha. The couches are quite comfortable, and they serve quality tea.

148 CYAN

9737 Yonge St
Richmond Hill ⑪
ON L4C 8S7
+1 905 237 4266
cyancafe.com

Cyan is more than a shisha lounge. The food is good, and they also serve liquor. The vibe is more modern Middle Eastern than in other lounges. Cyan also invites DJs and performers on weekends, who play a mix of Middle Eastern and North American music.

149 HABIBI LOUNGE

2921 Derry Road E
Mississauga ⑧
ON L4T 1A6
+1 905 956 6333
habibi-lounge-halal-
restaurant.business.site

Habibi Lounge is a smaller and quieter lounge. Its red and dark wood decor is inviting. Guests are welcomed to this family-owned establishment with a smile. Some spots within the lounge feel like you are sitting in your living room. It's a good place to chill for an evening.

150 ALI BASHA

147 Dundas St E
Downtown ①
+1 647 606 9939

Ali Basha is one of the few shisha bars right in the city. It's a low-key spot with reasonable prices. Ali Basha is not a high-end shisha lounge; it's a bit gritty but comfortable and filled with locals who like to make shisha a daily habit.

TINY RECORD SHOP

55 PLACES
TO SHOP

---

5 places to experience all that is great about **CHINATOWN**

151 **LUCKY MOOSE**
393 Dundas St W
Downtown ①
+1 416 351 8688
lmfoodmart.com

There are two reasons to visit Lucky Moose. The first is the fun moose statue that stands above the entranceway. It's one of many you will find throughout the city. The second is that it is filled to the rafters with good deals. You'll find Chinese groceries beside North American cookie brands.

152 **HUA SHENG SUPERMARKET**
293 Spadina Avenue
Downtown ①
+1 416 263 9883

Hua Sheng is probably as close to China as you can get in Canada. The store is packed with produce items. The packaging is almost always in Chinese. They have fresh fish and meat counters, and their prices are known throughout the neighbourhood to be the lowest.

153 **CHINATOWN DOLLAR MART**
490 Dundas St W
Downtown ①
+1 416 977 6362

It's basic, it's a dollar store, but it's filled with all sorts of weird and wonderful trinkets. It is very much a part of the Chinatown vibe and worth a visit just for the experience.

154 TAP PHONG

360 Spadina Avenue
Downtown ⓘ
+1 416 977 6364
tapphong.com

Tap Phong has everything you need for your kitchen. They sell wholesale products so you can find some really good deals on kitchen items. The store, like most of Chinatown, is packed with merchandise. It's fun to wander through the aisles.

155 DRAGON CITY MALL

280 Spadina Avenue
Downtown ⓘ

Dragon City Mall is a unique visit. It's full of Chinese stores selling all sorts of items. A lot of Chinese-speaking locals hang out inside the mall. There are lots of little stores to peruse, along with a tasty dim sum restaurant on the top floor.

CHINATOWN

The 5 best independent
BOOKSTORES
for the book nerd

---

156 MONKEY'S PAW

1067 Bloor St W
Midtown ③
+1 416 531 2123
monkeyspaw.com

Monkey's Paw is about old and unusual books. You won't find Harry Potter here, but you might find a whole book about edible mushrooms. They have this cool Biblio-Mat, which is an old book vending machine. It dispenses random old books for about a *twoonie*.

157 TYPE BOOKS

157 TYPE BOOKS

883 Queen St W
Downtown ⓘ
+1 416 366 8973
typebooks.ca

Type Books has several locations in the GTA, but they began here at this location in Trinity Bellwoods. It's a bright store that feels comfortable as soon as you step through the door. They have all the mainstream titles as well as lots of local authors.

158 GLAD DAY BOOKSHOP

499 Church St
Downtown ⓘ
+1 416 901 6600
www.gladday
bookshop.com

Glad Day is the world's oldest bookstore focusing on LGBTQ literature. It's a funky spot that's more than just a bookstore. They recently moved to this location and added a restaurant. On weekends they hold dance parties in the shop. Walking into Glad Day will give a good feel for the type of vibe in the Church and Wellesley neighbourhood.

159 ANOTHER STORY BOOKSHOP

315 Roncesvalles Ave
West End ⑥
+1 416 462 1104
anotherstory.ca

Another Story is one of those stores that locals keep coming back to time and again. The store focuses on books about social justice, so many of the titles found here will be quite informative. If you love thought-provoking reads, you'll love this place.

160 THE BEGUILING

319 College St
Downtown ⓘ
+1 416 533 9168
beguilingbooks
andart.com

They focus on selling graphic novels and comics. The employees are all passionate about the genre and will help you to find the right book. I've spent hours perusing their novels with the help of the staff. If you have children, visit their sister store, Little Island Comics.

The 5 best shops to find
ARTISAN GOODS

161 STACKT MARKET

28 Bathurst St
Downtown ①
stacktmarket.com

The Stackt Market is a new complex near Fort York, built entirely of shipping containers. Some vendors are permanent, others are temporary pop-up shops. The market features artists, craft brewers and other locally made products. They often have activities for kids.

162 LIKELY GENERAL

389 Roncesvalles Ave
West End ⑥
+1 647 351 4590
likelygeneral.com

Likely has it all. It's basically a general store, but what sets it apart is that every product is ethically sourced or locally made. There's everything from honey to lip balm, clothing and art. It's a super fun store to visit, and the owner prides herself on stocking great items you won't find in other places.

163 HART & HIVE

353 College St
Downtown ①
+1 647 812 1022
hartandhive.com

Hart & Hive began when the owner graduated from Design College and struggled to find a place to sell his handmade items. He founded this store and stocked it with his creations along with those of other Canadian designers and makers. The handbags are beautiful pieces of art.

164 ELEPHANT IN THE ATTIC

1596 Dundas St W
West End ⑥
+1 416 532 4350
elephantintheattic.ca

Elephant in the Attic is listed on Yelp as an art gallery. It is a gallery, but one with a twist. The store is organized into mini-exhibitions, which all follow a theme. Items in the exhibitions range from framed art to jewellery and all sorts of other items.

165 THE SHOP

1485 Dupont St,
Unit 113
West End ⑥
+1 416 414 7764
theshoptoronto.ca

The Shop is a full-service maker studio. You can head in and make your own pottery. They sell day passes, but you can also purchase a monthly pass. It's also fun to watch others create and talk about ideas. Many of the makers sell their pottery, too.

161 STACKT MARKET

5 shops where you'll find
UNIQUE SOUVENIRS

166 THE SOUVENIR MARKET
AT: ST. LAWRENCE MARKET
91 Front St E
Downtown ①
+1 416 203 0033
thesouvenirmarket.com

If you want to find a cheap souvenir of your time here in Toronto, this market has it all. You can pick up RCMP memorabilia (Royal Canadian Mounted Police) or a small jar of maple syrup. This tiny store has a ton of items for everyone. It's also the meeting place for several walking tours.

167 DRAKE GENERAL STORE
AT: THE DRAKE HOTEL
1150 Queens St W
West End ⑥
+1 416 538 2222
drakegeneralstore.ca

The Store is located in The Drake Hotel. It's a general store with something for everyone. The items are a little less mainstream than your typical souvenirs. You can find some pretty cool Blue Jays T-shirts as well as locally created Toronto Raptors art.

168 BLUE BANANA MARKET
250 Augusta Avenue
Downtown ①
+1 416 594 6600
bluebananamarket.com

The Blue Banana is just one of those places you have to visit if you're in Kensington Market, as it's a neighbourhood icon. It's a large store with a lot of gadgets, all reasonably priced. My personal favourite are the funky socks, many of which are Canadian themed.

169 **SHOPAGO**
AT: ART GALLERY
OF ONTARIO, LEVEL 1
317 Dundas St W
Downtown ①
shop.ago.ca/store

The AGO is the Met of Toronto. While the Met may have a larger store, the AGO certainly has a similar amount of variety. You'll find a lot of small prints and postcards highlighting Canadian artists, as well as high-quality jewellery.

170 **SPACING STORE**
401 Richmond St W
Downtown ①
+1 416 644 1017
spacingstore.ca

Spacing Store has published a line of books focused on Toronto and its quirks and wonderfulness. The line of books is informative and fun to peruse. Topics include etiquette, transit secrets, Toronto Raptors memories and a variety of other topics. You won't find these books anywhere else.

170 SPACING STORE

5

MALLS AND OUTLETS

where you can spend an afternoon

---

171 PACIFIC MALL

4300 Steeles Ave E
Markham ⑦
ON L3R 0Y5
+1 905 470 8785
pacificmalltoronto.ca

Pacific Mall is a huge Asian shopping centre. There are lots of typical vendors. You'll also find a touristy heritage town located on the second floor. It's a bit of a tourist trap, but it also feels like a traditional Asian market – not a bad activity on a rainy day.

172 CF SHOPS AT DON MILLS

1090 Don Mills Road
North York ④
+1 416 447 6087
cfshops.com/shops-at-don-mills.html

Don Mills has all the typical stores you'd find in any mall. It's a larger location, so there are lots of shops to peruse. They have an indoor mini-train for kids. The tickets are only 4 dollar each, which isn't expensive for a gimmicky ride.

173 SQUARE ONE SHOPPING CENTRE

100 City Centre Drive
Mississauga ⑧
ON L5B 2C9
+1 905 270 7771
shopsquareone.com

This is a busy shopping centre filled with a full range of stores. It's also in the heart of Mississauga. There are some unique buildings nearby as well as Mississauga town hall, which is quite pretty. You can send the kids to Playdium and go shopping in peace.

174 **BAYVIEW VILLAGE SHOPS**

2901 Bayview Avenue
North York ⓝ
+1 416 226 0404
bayviewvillage
shops.com

Bayview is a high-end shopping establishment in the heart of Bayview Village. It's quite elegant inside. There are areas with crystal chandeliers and fancy carpets. Most stores cater to the affluent of society, but it is fun to window-shop here.

175 **DIXIE OUTLET MALL**

1250 South Service Rd
Mississauga ⑧
ON L5E 1V4
+1 905 278 3494
dixieoutletmall.com

Dixie Outlet is not a high-end posh shopping centre. It's a little dingy and aged, full of discount stores and cluttered outlets. There's a nice flea market located in the basement: you'll find everything from T-shirts to used CDs at the under-ground level.

The 5 most unique
ANTIQUE *and* SALVAGE SHOPS

176 PASSION FOR THE PAST ANTIQUES & COLLECTIBLES

1646 Queen St W
West End ⑥
+1 416 535 3883
*passionforthepast
antiques.com*

Located in Parkdale, Passion For The Past carries everything antique. It's a mishmash of everything from ladies' jewellery to silverware. The owners are knowledgeable and will help you find just the right items.

177 BLACKBIRD VINTAGE FINDS

11 Trinity St
Downtown ①
+1 416 681 0558
blackbirdvintage.com

Blackbird Vintage is located in the Distillery District. It carries lots of great antiques. The owner likes to find local historical items. The location is a plus: you can visit this store along with a collection of art galleries, then head to the Mill Pub for a craft brew.

178 SMASH SALVAGE

371 Sherman Ave N
Hamilton ⑨
ON L8L 6N2
+1 416 809 8730
smashsalvage.com

Smash Salvage specializes in salvaged furniture and lighting. They have other items as well, but furniture is their specialty. The items are very trendy, and the staff have a good eye for design. They are happy to help you create a look for your home.

179 RANSACK THE UNIVERSE

1207 Bloor St W
Midtown ③
+1 647 703 6675

The name says it all. This store is about finding anything and everything weird and wonderful from the past. They've got lots of furniture as well as old wedding dresses and some very odd finds, like mannequin heads.

180 A CHANGING NEST

572 Annette St
West End ⑥
+1 416 519 2011
achangingnest.com

A Changing Nest caters to those looking to refine their space with antique and salvage finds. It's a cluttered store, but everything is artfully arranged. This is a place filled with eye candy. The owner is passionate about beautiful design. She offers design-consulting services.

The top 5
VINYL RECORD STORES

---

181 SONIC BOOM

215 Spadina Avenue
Downtown ①
+1 416 532 0334
sonicboommusic.com

Sonic Boom is a huge record store. They've got everything from brand-new releases to old records from the 1970s. They also have a collection of books on sale. If you're a music lover, this is a place to visit. They take records and sound quality very seriously.

182 TINY RECORD SHOP

182 TINY RECORD SHOP

777 Queen St E
East End ⑤
+1 416 479 4363
tinyrecordshop.com

This place will purchase your entire record collection if you wish to sell it. They are smaller than Sonic Boom but just as knowledgeable. The store is neatly arranged, and it's easy to find all your favourite artists. The staff is friendly and helpful.

183 ROTATE THIS

186 Ossington Ave
Downtown ①
+1 416 504 8447
rotate.com

Rotate This has been open for over 25 years. Everyone who is into vinyl knows about this place. They carry all genres except country and classical. The staff love music and like to have fun. The vibe is obvious when you step into the store. You can also pick up tickets to local concerts here.

184 KOPS RECORDS

229 Queen St W
Downtown ①
+1 647 347 0095
kopsrecords.ca

Kops Records is another giant in the Toronto record scene, with three locations throughout the city. They know their records and will buy and sell very carefully. The owner has been in the record business for over 40 years. He prides himself on the ethical buying and selling of records.

185 PANDEMONIUM

2920 Dundas St W
West End ⑥
+1 416 769 5257
pandemonium.ca

Pandemonium sells records, CDs, books, DVDs and art. The store has mostly used items. They are picky, so if you're looking to sell some of your items, make sure you only bring pieces that are in really good condition.

5

MARKETS

to explore

---

186 SORAUREN FARMERS' MARKET
50 Wabash Avenue
West End ⑥
sosaurenmarket.com

Sorauren operates on Mondays from 3 to 7 pm. The timing makes it accessible to a lot of people, because it allows you to pick up some produce after work. Some people head to the park and pick up snacks for dinner while their kids play. It's a family-oriented market.

187 CABBAGETOWN FARMERS' MARKET
AT: RIVERDALE PARK WEST
191 Winchester St
Downtown ①
cabbagetownmarket.ca

The Cabbagetown Market runs from June to October and is located in Riverdale Park West. It's a pretty spot to visit on a Tuesday evening. The view of the city will be a nice bonus to your visit. There's a crepe vendor, Vanilla DC. Head there to pick up dessert.

188 NATHAN PHILLIPS SQUARE FARMERS' MARKET
100 Queen St W
Downtown ①

This is a big market, centrally located in downtown Toronto. People often pop out of offices to purchase their lunch here. Open Wednesdays from 8 am to 3 pm from May to October. There is also a stage where bands perform during the market. They usually have family events planned as well.

189 GERRARD INDIA BAZAAR

Gerrard St E
between Glenside
and Coxwell
East End ⑤
gerrardindiabazaar.com

The Bazaar is more of a series of planned events and sales than a farmers' market. All events are timed with different Indian celebrations. Not only do local vendors sell their wares, but each event is meant to help promote Indian culture and Canadian diversity. Always a lot of fun.

190 EVERGREEN BRICK WORKS' FARMERS' MARKET

550 Bayview Avenue
East York ④
+1 416 596 1495
evergreen.ca

The Brick Works' market is open on Saturdays from 8 am to 1 pm. It's another huge market, perhaps the largest in Toronto. The Brick Works fiercely promotes environmental sustainability. You'll find lots of local vendors with everything from handmade items to organic produce. There are often activities for children, too.

190 EVERGREEN BRICK WORKS' FARMERS' MARKET

5 great places to purchase
LOCAL FOODS

191 THE BIG CARROT

348 Danforth Ave
East End ⑤
+1 416 466 2129
thebigcarrot.ca

The Big Carrot is a natural food store. It's been a part of the community for close to 20 years. They source local produce as well as natural and organic products. The store is very much community-oriented. You can call ahead to arrange a tour of the store.

192 FRESH FROM THE FARM

350 Donlands Ave
East York ④
+1 416 422 3276
freshfromthefarm.ca

This store sources its products from local Mennonite families. The goal of the partnership is to provide local Torontonians with fresh produce that meets their ethical standards. It also offers Mennonites an opportunity to access the city market place, as many Mennonites don't use motorized vehicles. This way, the store creates a bridge between communities.

193 KARMA CO-OP

799 Palmerstone Ave
Midtown ③
+1 416 534 1470
karmacoop.org

Karma may be an option if you're staying in town for an extended amount of time. It's a local food cooperative. You can purchase a membership and shop here. They have several different types of memberships to suit everyone's needs.

194 RAISE THE ROOT

1164 Queen St E
East End ⑤
+1 416 466 7668
raisetheroot.ca

Raise the Root sells local organic produce for as much of the season as is possible. The store is so cute. There are tasty items located on shelves everywhere. They offer artisanal bread as well as fresh produce. You will also find locally made jarred food like pasta sauces.

195 THE SWEET POTATO

108 Vine Avenue
West End ⑥
+1 416 762 4848
thesweetpotato.ca

The Sweet Potato feels like a big-box grocery store, but it isn't. It's an independent grocer. You will find everything you need here. The store focuses on organic and local produce, including a meat counter and bakery. There's a small seating area where you can enjoy pre-made sandwiches.

4 FLORISTS *and 1 big* FLOWER MARKET

all worth browsing

---

196 YANG'S FLOWER AND FRUIT MARKET

132 Avenue Road
Midtown ③
+1 416 413 9195

There are several flower shops on Avenue Road, and Yang's is one of the most colourful ones. Walking into the store is like walking into a rainbow. They have lots of orchids as well as fresh-cut flowers, and they specialize in tropical and Asian flowers. The owner is very knowledgeable.

197 KEN'S FLOWERS ON AVENUE ROAD

130 Avenue Road
Midtown ③
+1 647 341 4536
kensflowerson
avenue.com

Ken's Flowers is a neat and tidy shop. The flowers are arranged according to type. It's a beautiful scene to walk into, with so much vibrant colour. They specialize in arrangements and are happy to work with you to create the perfect arrangement.

198 JONG YOUNG FLOWER MARKET

128 Avenue Road
Midtown ③
+1 416 922 4421
jongyoung
flowermarket.ca

Located in an area where flower shops seem to congregate, Jong Young prides itself on being a picky flower provider. They ensure that the quality of their selection is extremely high. The shop feels a lot like a greenhouse when you walk in. They have buckets of fresh-cut flowers, as well as potted plants.

199 GROWER'S FLOWER MARKET & GIFTS

126 Avenue Road
Midtown ③
+1 416 920 2442
growersflower.com

Grower's has an extensive list of bouquets you can pre-order. They've got lots of beautiful arrangements as well as fresh-cut flowers. It's easy to order from their website, but then you miss the experience of wandering through the store and enjoying all the perfumed scents of the ceiling-to-floor flowers.

200 TORONTO FLOWER MARKET

AT: CAMH PARKING –
SHAW ST ENTRANCE
1001 Queen St W
Downtown ①
torontoflower
market.ca

Located in the CAMH parking lot, this flower market isn't a bricks-and-mortar store. Instead, you can peruse a variety of stalls from different sellers. The market runs from May to October, and visiting the flower market in spring after a dreary winter is probably one of the most uplifting times for locals. Check the website for market dates.

5 great
NEIGHBOURHOODS
for shopping

201 **CASTLEFIELD DESIGN DISTRICT**

Northeast of
Dufferin St and
Eglinton Ave
York-Crosstown ③

The area near Dufferin and Eglinton hosts a variety of design stores. If you're looking for furniture or home decor items, this is a good area to visit. Stores like Elte and Metropolis Living are situated within walking distance of each other. Take a wander around and find trendy designs.

202 **BLOOR-YORKVILLE**

Between Avenue
Road and Yonge St,
north of Bloor St W
Midtown ③
bloor-yorkville.com

Bloor-Yorkville isn't a neighbourhood in which you'll find a lot of discount stores. This area is known for all its high-end stores. There's a Louis Vuitton, Holt Renfrew, 119 Corbo, Chanel and Nordstrom located within walking distance of each other. There are also nice boutique stores here.

203 YONGE-EGLINTON

Uptown ③

The Yonge and Eglinton area is about 2 kilometres in radius and filled with lots of shops offering designer labels for adults and children. It's also home to the Yonge-Eglinton Shopping Centre, so lots of spots where you can empty your wallet. It's best to start at the intersection of Yonge and Eglinton Avenue West, then take your time wandering both east and west along the corridor.

204 RONCESVALLES VILLAGE

Roncesvalles Ave
from the Gardiner
to Bloor St W
West End ⑥
roncesvallesvillage.ca

Roncesvalles is far less pretentious than Bloor and Yonge. There are lots of little boutique shops here where you can find one-off items. Wander straight down 'Roncy', and you will find lots of little places that catch your eye and pique your curiosity.

205 THE BEACHES

Queen St E from
Woodbine Park to
Victoria Park Ave
East End ⑤

The Beaches has a vibe that's totally different from other parts of the city. It has a lovely art community as well as some high-end shopping. There's also this down-to-earth feel to the Beaches. You find lots of stores with reasonably priced items as well. Its a mix of both worlds.

THE NARWHAL BOUTIQUE

55 PLACES
FOR FASHION
AND DESIGN

The 5 best places to purchase local
CANADIAN DESIGN

206 VITALY ON YONGE

350 Yonge St
Downtown ⓘ
+1 416 519 3967
vitalydesign.ca

Vitaly has skyrocketed since they appeared on a Canadian TV show called *Dragons' Den*. The company has quickly become known for creating edgy unisex-designed jewellery and accessories. They began by creating wooden jewellery and then switched to stainless steel as their main material.

207 HAYLEY ELSAESSER

695 Queen St W
Downtown ⓘ
+1 416 223 4400
hayleyelsaesser.com

Hayley Elsaesser creates fun and quirky fashion. Describing her own designs as bold, colourful and busy, she creates pieces that get noticed. It's not the type of clothing you would wear to a black-tie event. Her designs appeal to a lot of young Torontonians.

208 COAL MINER'S DAUGHTER

744 Queen St W
Downtown ⓘ
coalminersdaughter.ca

The Coal Miner's Daughter carries a variety of Canadian-made designs. You'll find items from other parts of the world as well, but they like to focus on local design. There are five locations throughout the GTA. They sell clothing and accessories, as well as a small selection of beauty products.

209 **18 WAITS**

990 Queen St W
Downtown ①
+1 647 346 0118
18waits.com

18 Waits can best be described as a very cool men's clothing store. The owner is a designer and you will find bolts of cloth leaning against the wall. His patterns hang in the back change room. He sells a neat selection of boys clothing as well.

210 **ELEVEN THIRTY SHOP**

1130 College St
West End ⑥
+1 416 588 1130
eleventhirtyshop.com

Eleven Thirty was founded by two friends with a passion for design. The front of the store works as a regular retail enterprise, and the back of the store is their design studio; all leather bags are made in-house. They've just started selling clothing as well.

209 **18 WAITS**

5 independent
JEWELLERY
DESIGNERS

---

211 JENNY BIRD

174 Spadina Ave
Downtown ①
+1 647 346 2473
jenny-bird.ca

Jenny Bird is a well-known jewellery designer who has her flagship store in Toronto. Her designs can be found throughout the world. She works primarily in gold and silver, creating simple and elegant designs. The store is filled with lots of eye candy. She likes to call her regulars 'Birdgirls'.

212 MADE YOU LOOK

1338 Queen St W
West End ⑥
+1 416 463 2136
madeyoulook.ca

Made You Look is a large, popular store that's actually more of a collective. You'll find a huge number of designers under one roof, many of whom work right in store. They have everything from wedding bands to hoop earrings. It's all high-end jewellery, and the quality is evident.

213 STUDIO 1098

1098 Yonge St
Midtown ③
+1 416 944 1098
studio1098
customjewellery.com

Studio 1098 specializes in making custom designs. They will sit down with you and work to create the perfect item. They do sell pre-made items as well, but most people visit this studio for their custom work. The staff is very responsive to client needs.

214 ANNE SPORTUN

742 Queen St W
Downtown ①
+1 416 363 4114
annesportun.com

Anne Sportun is a big name in Canadian jewellery. She's been in business since 1980. Her work is found in high-quality jewellery stores around the world. The flagship store is refined and elegant. There's a sense of calm and elegance to the decor, which is reflected in the designs.

215 ARMED

1380 Queen St W
West End ⑥
+1 437 221 1063
upandarmed.com

Armed is a smaller store selling items in the more affordable range for most people. Their jewellery is fun and edgy and is handmade by the designer. She makes the cutest little charm necklaces. The pieces are unique and eye-catching.

212 MADE YOU LOOK

The 5 funkiest boutiques to find
UNIQUE CLOTHING

---

216 UNCLE OTIS

329 Spadina Avenue
Downtown ⓘ
+1 416 920 2281
uncleotis.com

Uncle Otis is one of the coolest men's stores out there. Brands are sourced from around the world. The clothing is casual and more focused on providing younger crowds with comfortable streetwear. Think button-down shirts in patterns or plaids, and lots of khakis and jeans with running shoes.

217 PINK CANARY

280 Augusta Avenue
Downtown ⓘ
+1 647 495 2479
pinkcanary.com

Pink Canary is packed with tons of different styles. The owner finds brands in cities like LA and New York. Prices are fairly reasonable, and they bring in new styles almost every week. You'll find lots of dresses great for a night out, as well as jeans and T-shirts.

218 THE FERAL

890 Queen St W
Downtown ⓘ
+1 647 346 0144
theferal.me

The Feral is a clothing line by Toronto-based designer Zakariah Milana. His clothing is moody, edgy and unconventional. You won't find any bright colours here. The designs are almost gothic, with lots of greys and blacks.

219 6 BY GEE BEAUTY

6 Roxborough St W
Midtown ③
+1 416 960 8080
6bygeebeauty.com

Opened by the pair of women who run Gee Beauty, this little boutique provides shoppers with luxury travel essentials. They have a nice range of clothing and sunglasses. One of my favourite reasons to visit is the perfume bar. There's always something lovely to test.

220 THE NARWHAL BOUTIQUE

1128 Yonge St
Midtown ③
+1 647 351 5011
narwhalboutique.com

This boutique is fun. The clothes are comfortable and relaxed. It has a very bohemian style, with lots of loose flowy dresses and bright colours. Many of the pieces are quite pricey, but if you arrive during a sale you can get some really great quality clothing for a respectable price.

220 THE NARWHAL BOUTIQUE

5 places to find
VINTAGE CLOTHING

---

221 CHOSEN VINTAGE
1599 Dundas St W
West End ⑥
+1 647 346 1993
chosen-vintage.com

Chosen Vintage is one of those second-hand stores where quality is important. They're picky about the items they sell. You won't find 1-dollar-discount racks in this store. You might however come across a men's tux from the 1930s or a beautiful vintage dress that screams: "BUY ME!"

222 PENNY ARCADE
1177 Dundas St W
Downtown ①
+1 647 346 1386
pennyarcade
vintage.com

Penny Arcade is just a cool store. The owner is very particular about the items she sells. The pieces are often restored and in mint condition. She also sells a variety of different handmade pieces by local Toronto designers, and some beautiful handmade swimsuits and lingerie.

223 PUBLIC BUTTER
1290 Queen St W
Downtown ②
+1 416 535 4343
publicbutter.com

Public Butter has everything. Yes, it's a vintage clothing store, but they also have salvaged goods. You'll find secondhand bikes next to piles of cowboy boots. The clothing is all in pretty good shape. You'll enjoy sifting through the variety of items in this store.

224 HOUSE OF VINTAGE

1239 Queen St W
West End ⑥
+1 416 535 2142

House of Vintage is a pretty little store located in Parkdale. The quality of the clothing is excellent. They focus on selling designer brands. All items are beautifully presented, and it's easy to put together a nice outfit as you stroll through the store.

225 SIBERIA VINTAGE

955 Bloor St W
Midtown ③
+1 416 476 5152

Siberia Vintage is another vintage store that carefully curates the clothes they offer. Everything in the store is organized by colour. The owner seems to have found some of the most beautiful dresses from the 1970s and 1980s. They only sell women's clothing.

5
SECONDHAND STORES
to dig through

---

226 COFFEE AND CLOTHING

348 Pape Avenue
East End ⑤
+1 647 336 8546
coffeeandclothing.ca

Coffee and Clothing is exactly what its name says. It's an odd mix of a cafe and a secondhand store. It's a nice mix though. Take your time shopping then enjoy a coffee on the back patio. It's of those stores with tons of character.

227 GADABOUT

1300 Queen St E
East End ⑤
+1 416 463 1254
gadaboutvintage.com

Gadabout is in the secondhand list and not the vintage list because this store offers so much more than clothing. They carry everything from vintage fashion to obscure treasures like a collection of Russian *matryoshka* dolls. The store is packed from floor to ceiling with impressive finds.

228 BLACK MARKET

347 Queen St W
Downtown ①
+1 416 599 5858
blackmarket toronto.com

Black Market is about finding it cheap. They have racks of clothes for 10 dollar or less. Packed full of items, it will take time to sift through everything. Black Market is not the place to come when searching for a fancy high-class shopping experience. Its eclectic and a little bit wild.

229 COMMON SORT

1414 Queen St W
West End ⑥
+1 416 463 7678
commonsort.com

Common Sort is a classic thrift shop.
They buy-sell, and trade used clothing.
They are picky about what they sell
and everything is on consignment.
Nevertheless, it's a great place to shop.
This store is about finding the hidden
gems, but you will need time to sift
through their huge offering.

230 COURAGE MY LOVE

14 Kensington Ave
Downtown ①
+1 416 979 1992

Courage My Love is just a cool store,
with lots of cheap finds. You can pick
up items from their 5-dollar rack or take
the time to wander through the store and
search for whatever catches your eye.
They often have some very nice vintage
dish sets available.

The 5 most awesome
TATTOO PARLOURS

---

231 INK & WATER TATTOO
1303 Bloor St W
West End ⑥
+1 416 000 1599
inkandwatertattoo.ca

Ink & Water focuses on custom tattooing. Each design is unique to the individual. The shop is not your usual gritty tattoo parlour. It feels more like you're walking into a spa or a high-end clothing store. The vibe is welcoming and friendly.

232 HOLY NOIR
790 Dundas St W
Downtown ①
holynoir.com

Holy Noir is my favourite tattoo parlour. They have several artists working here. Each has her own unique style but the work is impeccable. This is one of the few female-owned parlours in the city.

233 CHRONIC INK
378 Yonge St
Downtown ①
+1 416 341 0311
chronicinktattoo.com

Chronic Ink is a large tattoo studio that also offers piercing and microblading. They have a second shop in Vancouver, and the name has become well known. They're famous for their full-body tattoos and custom work. They also have an impressive portfolio of Asian tattoos.

234 SPEAKEASY TATTOO

299 Harbord St
Downtown ①
+1 647 378 2481
speakeasy-tattoo.com

Speakeasy is a small laidback tattoo parlour. There are lovely bright colours on the wall, and it's easy to feel comfortable here. They have a strict 18+ policy that speaks to the integrity of the shop. The multitude of art means you can pick the style you like.

235 PASSAGE TATTOO

80 Geary Avenue
Midtown ③
passagetattoo.com

Passage Tattoo has been in business in Toronto for 20 years. The owner is well known and proud of the many apprentices he has trained, who have moved on to open their own tattoo parlours. Passage has a more traditional feel to it. The space is filled with natural light, and classics are designed here.

5

MEN'S FASHION

stores to visit

---

236 LAVISH & SQUALOR

253 Queen St W
Downtown ①
+1 416 530 0003
*themerchants
general.com*

Lavish & Squalor sells both men's and women's clothes, but the store has a masculine feel to it. The inside feels like a rustic cottage and they also have a coffee bar. You'll find the store is stocked with comfy plaid shirts. They sell a nice line of beauty products, too.

237 CNTRBND

135 Yorkville Avenue
Midtown ③
+1 416 928 1414
cntrbndshop.com

Located in Yorkville, this store will be heavy on your wallet. They carry lots of great brands, and the store feels like a relaxed upscale New York-type of store. Items are arranged in an attractive manner when you enter the store, and it's easy to find what you need.

238 SYDNEY'S

682 Queen St W
Downtown ①
+1 416 603 3369
shopsydneys.com

Sydney's offers made-to-measure men's suits plus a large selection of other menswear. Many of the items are made in-house while others are sourced from local Canadian designers. Every man who walks out of Sydney's seems to exude a classic suave aura. It must be the clothes.

239 KORRY'S CLOTHIERS

569 Danforth Ave
East End ⑤
+1 416 463 1115
korrys.com

Korry's is an icon on Danforth. The store is well known throughout the city. They often advertise on local radio. The owner participates in the ads, and they've become a part of the fabric of Toronto. The store sells higher-end brands of suits and clothing for men.

240 OUTCLASS

343 Roncesvalles Ave
West End ⑥
outclass.ca

Outclass sells only Canadian-made garments. The designer is focused on providing classically styled menswear that feels modern. The store is filled with button-down shirts and khaki-type pants. The look transfers easily from daytime workday to nighttime fun.

The 5 most
UNUSUAL SHOPS *in* TO

241 **WEIRD THINGS**
998 Bathurst St
Midtown ③
+1 647 786 2987

Weird Things carries, well, weird items. This antique/art gallery is tucked away on a quieter section of Bathurst. You never know what you'll find inside. It's worth a look if you like discovering strange little treasures that will make your friends ask questions.

245 KID ICARUS

242 CURIOSA

1273 Queen St W
West End ⑥
+1 647 341 0394
curiosasociety.com

Curiosa is a Harry Potter-themed store. When you enter the store, you will feel like you've walked onto the set of a Harry Potter movie. The owner proudly explains how the various items relate to different characters from the movie. If you're a fan, this is the place to shop.

243 DOLL FACTORY BY DAMZELS

394 Roncesvalles Ave
West End ⑥
+1 416 533 3232
damzels.com

This store supplies Toronto with a multitude of vintage-inspired dresses. If you're looking for something that screams June Cleaver from the 1950s TV show, this is the place to visit. The dresses are pretty, feminine and colourful.

244 SAUDADE

1191 Dundas St W
Downtown ①
+1 647 352 1191
saudadetoronto.com

Saudade is a home decor store, but it focuses on providing visitors with Portuguese-inspired design. The designs are traditional, for the most part. Some pieces in the store also reflect modern Portugal and an updated aesthetic.

245 KID ICARUS

205 Augusta Avenue
Downtown ①
+1 416 977 7236
kidicarus.ca

Kid Icarus is a screen-print shop. The printing area is open so you can watch designers work and create hand-printed works of art. They also sell these in-store creations, as well as other printed artwork made in Canada.

5 ARTS & CRAFTS
and DESIGN events
to wander through

246 TORONTO OUTDOOR ART FAIR

Nathan Phillips Square
Downtown ①
torontooutdoor.art

This is the biggest art fair around, with hundreds of vendors participating. The event fills almost all of Nathan Phillips Square and runs for three days every summer. The fair has been around for 58 years. You'll find lots of Canadian artists, photographers, potters, sculptures, etc.

247 KENSINGTON MARKET ART FAIR

77 Nassau St
Downtown ①
keep6.ca/kmaf

This art fair runs May to October and operates in the parking lot of a local bike shop. You'll find a mix of up-and-coming as well as established artists. The fair is timed to coincide with Pedestrian Sunday, which means you'll be walking the streets amidst a crowd of thousands.

248 NUIT BLANCHE
VARIOUS LOCATIONS THROUGHOUT THE GTA
toronto.ca/nbTO

Nuit Blanche is a major Toronto event. For one night, the streets fill with people celebrating, singing and visiting unique art exhibits. Some displays are set up on closed streets while others fill buildings. Most of the installations can be found in the downtown core, with some scattered throughout the rest of the city. Check the website for a map of the locations.

249 BEACHES ARTS & CRAFTS SHOW
AT: KEW GARDENS PARK
2075 Queen St E
East End ⑤
beachesartsandcraft
sshow.com

Kew Gardens is beautiful on its own, but when you add an art fair, it just makes the area more fun to visit. The fair is well established, and many artists set up shop there each year. The items are all made by locals, and they've carefully crafted their wares for sale.

250 CABBAGETOWN ART AND CRAFTS SALE
375 Sumach St
Downtown ①
cabbagetown
artandcrafts.org

This art fair is another small but well-established event. Lots of artisans apply each year for one of the spaces. Wander through the fair to find paintings, photography, pottery, handmade jewellery and lots of other artisan pieces.

The 5 best
SHOE STORES
to browse

---

251 **GET OUTSIDE**
437 Queen St W
Downtown ①
+1 416 593 5598
getoutsideshoes.com

Get Outside is an independent shoe retailer. They sell all the popular brands like Converse but in a smaller, more personal setting. Customer service is awesome and very patient. They want you to find just the right pair of shoes.

252 **JOHN FLUEVOG**
686 Queen St W
Downtown ①
+1 416 581 1420
fluevog.com

John Fluevog is one of those stores you have to visit for the experience. The store has been running since the 1970s. Many celebrities have worn Fluevog's shoes, and they proudly display this fact in their Flueseum. It's a unique experience as you learn about the history of this one-of-a-kind store.

253 **HEEL BOY**
773 Queen St W
Downtown ①
+1 416 362 4335
heelboy.com

Heel Boy has everything. The store's mission is to provide shoppers with a multi-generational experience. This means you will find unusual brands of shoes for every member of the family. The owner stocks specialty items as well as hard-to-find brands.

254 IMELDA

123 Roncesvalles Ave
West End ⑥
+1 647 344 1006
imelda.ca

Imelda is a store with lots of character.
They stock lovely comfortable brands for
women. The styles are very classic and
elegant. You can pick up a nice pair of
sandals for the beach as well as a pair
of runners for everyday outings.

255 LIVESTOCK

116 Spadina Avenue,
Unit G1
Downtown ①
+1 416 360 5483
deadstock.ca

You'll find Livestock in Toronto, Winnipeg
and Vancouver. It's a large store selling
shoes and clothing. They also stock
sporting brands, like Adidas, New Balance,
Converse and lots of others, making it the
place to come for running shoes.

252 JOHN FLUEVOG

5 shops with lots of
CASUAL WEAR

---

256 MUTTONHEAD

337 Roncesvalles Ave
West End ⑥
+1 647 341 4415
muttonheadstore.com

Muttonhead is the go-to store for locally made unisex athletic wear. The store has a funky vibe and is very much about items made to the concept of slow design. They do carry other Canadian brands, but all follow the same philosophy of quality and comfort.

257 MEC

300 Queen St W
Downtown ①
+1 416 340 2667
mec.ca

MEC is a Canadian outdoor giant. It is a cooperative; you must be a member to shop here. The good news is memberships only cost 5 dollar. The downtown store is big and bright, and carries a good selection of clothing and outdoor gear. They also have an in-store climbing wall.

258 ICEBREAKER TORONTO

278B Queen St W
Downtown ①
+1 416 596 9050
icebreaker.com

Icebreaker is an international outdoor-clothing store. The chain makes sustainable adventure wear, which is made using merino wool. The Toronto store is a nice bright place to visit and shop for the quality gear that you might need for exploring the wilds of Canada.

259 CAMOLOTS

184 Baldwin St
Downtown ①
+1 416 979 2266
camolots.com

This is North America, and if you're into outdoor pursuits, one of the best places to shop for deals is in an 'army navy' store. You'll find good-quality items mixed in with all the weird and wonderful items many surplus stores stock. And of course, lots and lots of camo gear.

260 ARC'TERYX

339 Queen St W
Downtown ①
+1 416 204 1118
arcteryx.com

Arc'teryx was founded in British Columbia and was designed for the active lifestyle many residents lead in this part of Canada. The Rocky Mountains make for a unique environment, and the clothing reflects the ever-changing weather conditions over there. This is the place to visit if you're into skiing.

256 / MUTTONHEAD

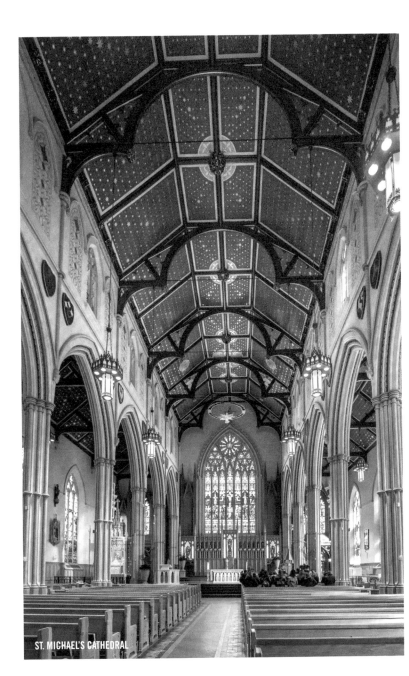
ST. MICHAEL'S CATHEDRAL

25 BUILDINGS TO ADMIRE

5

HISTORIC BUILDINGS
in TO

261 **ELGIN AND WINTER GARDEN THEATRE CENTRE**

189 Yonge St
Downtown ⓘ
+1 416 314 2901
*heritagetrust.on.ca/
en/ewg/ewg-home*

This theatre is pretty unique. It's a double-decker, the two stages were built one atop the other. Each platform is decorated differently and has its own personality. Constructed in 1913, the venues are filled with history. The organized tours are informative and reasonably priced. Cash only.

262 **COMMERCE COURT NORTH TOWER**

25 King St W
Downtown ⓘ
commercecourt.ca

Commerce Court is a very pretty spot. There are a fountain and sculptures, and going into the North Tower you get the chance to see some very beautiful art deco architecture. The ceiling of the banking hall is truly beautiful; it's six storeys tall.

263 **UNION STATION**

65 Front St W
Downtown ⓘ
torontounion.ca

Union Station is another art deco building located in the heart of Toronto. The main hall is huge, with arched ceilings and dim lighting. The front façade is quite pretty as well. The building is always under renovation, so be forewarned: your views may be partially blocked by scaffolding.

264 THE BLACK BULL

298 Queen St W
Downtown ①

The Black Bull is one of the oldest buildings in Toronto and the second-longest-running tavern in the city. The building has a lot of charm and was recently renovated due to a fire. The patio is a great spot to sit in summer.

265 R.C. HARRIS WATER TREATMENT PLANT

2701 Queen St E
East End ⑤

The water treatment centre is a true surprise. No one expects such a lavish art deco building for such a 'dirty' job. The ceilings are high, and there's plenty of light that flows through the building. You won't be able to visit the interior of the centre unless you are here during 'Doors Open Toronto' at the end of May. A walk around the exterior however is still a worthwhile effort.

The top 5
MODERN BUILDINGS
that make for great photographs

266 **ROYAL ONTARIO MUSEUM**
100 Queen's Park
Downtown ①
+1 416 586 8000
rom.on.ca

The ROM is a tourist hotspot, but with good reason. It's a complex of several buildings, all with different architectural styles. Some hate the complex because of the newest addition, the giant crystal entrance. You'll see what I mean: you either love it or hate it.

266 ROYAL ONTARIO MUSEUM

267 ROY THOMPSON HALL

60 Simcoe St
Downtown ①
+1 416 872 4255
roythomsonhall.com

From the exterior, Roy Thompson Hall reminds a little of an alien spaceship. The curved glass-like exterior glows in the sun. It's best to take photos of this building in the early morning or evening, as harsh light makes it difficult to photograph.

268 ART GALLERY OF ONTARIO – THE BACK WALL

317 Dundas St W
Downtown ①
+1 416 979 6648
ago.ca

The back wall of the AGO is a photographer's dream. There's a pretty park complete with water features, and a unique sculptural awning held up by coloured pencil pillars. The back of the building is like the ROM, a mix of older architecture and modern additions. It's beautiful.

269 ISMAILI CENTRE

49 Wynford Drive
North York ④
+1 416 646 6965
*the.ismaili/
ismailicentres/toronto*

The Ismaili Centre consists of a modern building, with a very pretty water feature right beside it. The grounds are lovely. This location is particularly good for anyone who likes to shoot night photography. The building glows with a warm light.

270 ARTSCAPE WESTON COMMON

34 John St
York-Crosstown ⑧
artscapeweston.ca

The exterior of this building is all about colour. That's what you'll be here for if you visit: you'll want to shoot the colourful façade. The area is a little gritty, but the brightness of this building makes everything much more interesting.

5 **AREAS** *worth exploring if you like* **ARCHITECTURE** *and* **ART**

---

271 **TORONTO ISLANDS**
Downtown ②

Spending the day wandering around the Toronto Islands can be a very pleasant experience. There's a small residential community with lots of pretty houses on Ward's Island. Centre Island has a lighthouse at Gibraltar Point and boasts a small amusement park. The area makes for amazing photographs.

272 **HUMBER BAY ARCH BRIDGE**
MARTIN GOODMAN TRAIL
West End ⑥

The Martin Goodman Trail follows the lakeshore and is a popular jogging route for locals. The bridge spanning the Humber River is an architectural beauty. You can take a moment to enjoy the scenery here as this is a pedestrian-only bridge. The parks on both sides of the river make for great picnic spots.

274 GRAFFITI ALLEY

273 UNIVERSITY OF TORONTO

27 King's College Circle
Downtown ⓘ
utoronto.ca

Toronto isn't old compared to many cities around the world. However, the university has a good concentration of heritage buildings, most of which date back to 1900. University College is a particularly beautiful site. It is one of the oldest on campus, dating back to 1859.

274 GRAFFITI ALLEY

Downtown ⓘ

Graffiti Alley is one of those spots worth taking a wander. The artwork is stunning. It may seem a little daunting to head down a rough-looking alley, but you'll be rewarded with colourful views. Some of the artwork is political, some of it's just plain silly, and some pieces are truly beautiful.

275 THE DISTILLERY DISTRICT

Downtown ⓘ

The Distillery District is quite touristy but with good reason. This pedestrian-only area of Toronto is full of beautiful heritage buildings. The old whiskey distillery has been converted into several art galleries. The cobblestone streets between the buildings are lined with interesting sculptures. You'll also find lots of great food to snack on in this area.

5 beautiful
SACRED PLACES
throughout Toronto

---

276 ST. PAUL'S BASILICA

83 Power St
Downtown ①
+1 416 364 7588
stpaulsbasilica.
archtoronto.org

St. Paul's feels like an old European church. The high arched ceilings are full of paintings in the style of the Italian Renaissance. The interior is painted white, so the space is very bright. Many locals book the church for weddings. The location makes for incredible and romantic photographs.

277 ST. MICHAEL'S CATHEDRAL

65 Bond St
Downtown ①
+1 416 364 0234
stmichaels
cathedral.com

In my opinion, the best time to see St. Mike's is in the evening, when the exterior is lit up by well-placed floodlights. The building seems to glow right around dusk. The interior is also stunning. There's a beautiful blue stained-glass window behind the main altar.

278 JAMI MOSQUE TORONTO

56 Boustead Avenue
West End ⑥
+1 416 769 1192
jamimosque.com

This is the oldest Islamic centre in Canada. The mosque is located in an old Presbyterian church. The arched ceiling is beautiful, and the walls have been painted white, which accents some of the old woodwork above it. The large Gothic doors at the entrance are quite pretty, too.

279 HOLY BLOSSOM TEMPLE

1950 Bathurst St
Midtown ③
+1 416 789 3291
holyblossom.org

Holy Blossom Temple has a lovely exterior entrance with large arches and a menorah adorning the wall. There's a bright, beautiful atrium inside the temple. You'll find the area filled with living green walls and a majestic curved staircase.

280 FUNG LOY KOK TAOIST TAI CHI – INTERNATIONAL CENTRE

248305 Side Road 5
Mono ⑪
ON L9W 6C3
+1 519 941 5981
taoist.org

Hidden in the hills of Mono, this Taoist temple is a surprise to most visitors. You will feel like you've walked into Taiwan or China when you first view the temple. Painted in bright reds and oranges, the building is a marvel. The interior is just as spectacular.

The 5 most **INTERESTING BUILDINGS** scattered throughout the city

---

281 **SHELDON & TRACY LEVY STUDENT LEARNING CENTRE**
AT: RYERSON UNIVERSITY

341 Yonge St
Downtown ①
+1 416 979 5000
ext.3485
slc.blog.ryerson.ca

This is a modern building. The exterior is a giant cube-like structure with an interesting and rather angular entrance-way. The ceiling just inside the entry doors has a unique geometrical pattern that will have you mesmerized by all the intricate lines and shapes it creates.

282 **ST. LAWRENCE MARKET**

93 Front St E
Downtown ①
+1 416 392 7219
stlawrencemarket.com

St. Lawrence Market is an old sprawling building with high ceilings. It's packed with indoor food stalls and candy vendors. The exterior resembles a sort of barn, with red brick accented by dark trim. I love the look of this place and the positive vibe everyone exudes while wandering through.

283 ARTSCAPE WYCHWOOD BARNS

601 Christie St
Midtown ③
+1 416 653 3520
*artscapewychwood
barns.ca*

Built in 1913, these 'barns' were originally used as a streetcar repair site. The buildings have been converted into a community centre, which is filled with artist studios. Many locals rent the venue for weddings. The large industrial entranceway is eye candy, as is the old stack rising above the roof.

284 THE REVUE CINEMA

400 Roncesvalles Ave
West End ⑥
+1 416 531 9950
revuecinema.ca

The Revue isn't large or grandiose, but it makes up for this shortfall in history. The building survived the depression of the 1930s and was occasionally used as a church during the Second World War. It is the oldest cinema in Toronto, and you can still watch films here.

285 BERGERON CENTRE
AT: YORK UNIVERSITY

11 Arboretum Lane
North York ⑪
+1 416 736 5484
thebergeroncentre.ca

The Bergeron Centre is a unique building. Its exterior reminds of puzzle pieces, but I think the architect was trying to create an abstracted version of a sky filled with white puffy clouds. It's located on the York University campus, so people won't mind if you wander around.

THE PASTURE

55 PLACES
TO DISCOVER
TORONTO

5 relaxing
WALKS in the **GTA**

286 **EVERGREEN BRICK WORKS**

550 Bayview Avenue
East York ④
+1 416 596 1495
ext.495
evergreen.ca

The Brick Works is all about the outdoors. On their website, you'll find a bunch of different trail maps that will lead you into the facility. They encourage you to leave your car behind and take an eco-friendly route onto the property. The Beltline Trail also runs through the property.

287 **PAN AM PATH**

From Brampton
Claireville Reservoir ⑧
to South of
Rouge Park ⑦
panampath.org

The Path was created to help celebrate the Pan Am Games, which visited Toronto in 2015. The trail runs the length of the GTA. This multi-use route is over 80 kilometres long. Check the website and choose a section you like. Along the route, you'll find lots of outdoor art installations.

288 **WEST TORONTO RAILPATH**

From Cariboo to
Strachan Avenue
West End ⑥
MG5X+G9
railpath.ca

This short walk utilizes an abandoned rail line and runs along the length of the Junction Triangle neighbourhood. It's multi-use and can easily be walked in 30 minutes. The trail extends 2 kilometres along the west Toronto region. You'll find temporary art displays along the path.

289 MIMICO WATERFRONT PARK

An evening stroll along the waterfront in Mimico is a pretty pleasant way to spend your time. The area connects nicely to the Humber Bay region. The multi-use trail is about 1 kilometre in length. The area has been carefully managed to ensure a natural habitat remains for wildlife.

290 GATES GULLY

The Doris McCarthy Trail running through Gates Gully was named after a famous Canadian painter. Her home, now an artist residency site, is located nearby. Wear good shoes when hiking here. The view is awesome from the top of the bluffs, and there's a sculpture at the bottom of the route near the lake.

286 EVERGREEN BRICK WORKS

5 places where you might
SPOT CELEBRITIES
during TIFF

---

291 THE RITZ-CARLTON
181 Wellington St W
Downtown ⓘ
+1 416 585 2500
ritzcarlton.com

It's the Ritz; it's fancy and exclusive. Of course, the celebrities will be here. Tons of movie stars have stayed here. The most recent was Ryan Gosling. The Ritz is open to the public, and there's a large terrace on the top floor where you can enjoy yourself while hoping to see someone famous.

292 THE SPOKE CLUB
600 King St W,
4th Floor
Downtown ⓘ
+1 416 368 8448
thespokeclub.com

The Spoke Club is a private members-only location. The club caters to young and hip creatives that are tied to the arts and media industries. It's a perfect spot for movie celebs. The likelihood of seeing a celebrity is high, but it will be fleeting as they head inside.

293 SOHO HOUSE
AT: BISHOP'S BUILDING
192 Adelaide St W
Downtown ⓘ
+1 416 599 7646
sohohousetoronto.com

Soho House is another exclusive club. They tend to host a large number of TIFF after-parties. This is the spot where you'll see celebrities converging to after movie showings. There are usually lots of people lined up here, hoping to catch a glimpse of someone famous.

294 MOMOFUKU TORONTO

190 University Ave
Downtown ⓘ
+1 647 253 6227
momofuku.com/
toronto

Momofuku is a famous restaurant in Toronto. It's part of the chain owned by celebrity chef David Chang. This location is open to the public but can often be closed during TIFF for private events. Some celebrities will quietly dine here, hoping to avoid drawing attention.

295 TIFF BELL LIGHTBOX

350 King St W
Downtown ⓘ
+1 416 599 2033
tiff.net

Of course, one of the best ways to see the celebrities is to hang around the Lightbox itself. There's a nice patio here, if you can get in during TIFF. The stars usually arrive with a ton of fanfare and paparazzi for the screenings of their films.

295 TIFF BELL LIGHTBOX

300 **SMOKEY HOLLOW**

The 5 most beautiful **WATERFALLS** *to visit near* **TO**

296 **ALBION FALLS**
PARKING LOT AT:
Arbour Road
Hamilton ⑨
ON L8W 3X9
cityofwaterfalls.ca/
albion-falls

Albion Falls is a really beautiful cascade that flows down the side of the Niagara Escarpment. The rock face is steep and can be slippery. This spot makes for amazing photographs, but go early in the day. The area can get busy with Instagram fanatics.

297 **BALL'S FALLS**
PARKING LOT AT:
BALL'S FALLS CENTRE
FOR CONSERVATION
3292 Sixth Avenue
Lincoln ⑩
ON L0R 1S0
+1 905 562 5235
npca.ca/parks/
balls-falls

Ball's Falls is located in a conservation area. You will need to pay admission here, but it's fairly cheap. The walk to the falls is well marked, and there are several historical buildings scattered around the property. The falls are big and loud and impressive. Also a good picnic spot.

298 CHEDOKE FALLS

Scenic Drive
Hamilton ⑨
ON L9C 1G5
*cityofwaterfalls.ca/
chedoke-falls*

Chedoke Falls lies on a well-travelled section of the Bruce Trail. The path is rocky, and follows along the bottom of the river gorge. It's a pretty hike, but wear good shoes. The path leads to the bottom of the falls and the small punch bowl of turquoise water. Beware: you won't be able to access the falls from Scenic Drive. You should go to the Chedoke Civic Golf Course and park at the far end of the parking lot. You then follow the trail along to the stairs.

299 DEVIL'S PUNCHBOWL

204 Ridge Road
Stoney Creek ⑨
ON L8J 2X4
*cityofwaterfalls.ca/
devils-punchbowl*

This fall is impressive. The bowl is huge, and the rock striations are beautiful. The amount of water flowing over the falls often drops to a trickle by late summer. The falls are located in a conservation area, so the hiking is fairly easy, but you have to pay admission.

300 SMOKEY HOLLOW

80 Mill St S
Hamilton ⑨
ON L0R 1R0
*tourismhamilton.com/
smokey-hollow*

This is one of the lesser-known falls in the area. It's a part of a 3-kilometre side-trail loop of the Bruce Trail. The hike is exhilarating; make sure you take a water bottle and snacks. A large amount of water flows over these 10-metre-high falls.

5 places to see
UNUSUAL SCULPTURES

---

301 **THE PASTURE**
BY JOSEPH FAFARD
Near Toronto
Dominion Centre
King and Bay St
Downtown ⓘ

It's a little odd when you're wandering through the financial district amidst the high-rise buildings, and all of a sudden the square opens up and seven life-sized cow sculptures are found resting in a quiet grassy area. It's a juxtaposition between city chaos and country calm.

302 **REMEMBERED SUSTENANCE**
BY CYNTHIA SHORT
55 John St
Downtown ⓘ

This sculpture consists of a series of 19 creatures that resemble cute rabbits/dogs. The animals are made of bronze and are located along a section of grass near a daycare. The artist wanted to evoke memories of childhood in the viewer by creating characters we might have seen in our imaginations.

303 RISING

BY ZHANG HUAN

188 University Ave
Downtown ①

This sculpture in front of the Shangri-La Hotel is one of my favourites in Toronto. The steel tree trunks twist and turn into the shape of a Chinese dragon, and are covered with birds. It's got a very magical and peaceful vibe to it. After viewing the sculpture, head up to the Shangri-La Lobby Lounge for a cocktail.

304 SCULPTURE HILL

Colborne Lodge Dr
West End ⑥
highparknature.org

Located in High Park, Sculpture Hill is a collection of 6 sculptures. The artworks were created by different artists from around the world. There are several paths that meander near the hill, so it's a nice walk to the top. The three yellow disks by Israeli artist Menashe Kadishman really stand out.

305 MEMORIAL TO THE WAR OF 1812

BY DOUGLAS COUPLAND

600 Fleet St
Downtown ②

To some Americans, this sculpture may be rather controversial. The sculpture depicts a Canadian soldier standing over an American soldier. The sculpture pays tribute to the war of 1812. Ask a Canadian, and they will say we won. Americans have a different opinion.

5 great spots for
SWIMMING

---

306 SUNNYSIDE – GUS RYDER OUTDOOR POOL

1755 Lake Shore Boulevard W
West End ⑥
toronto.ca

Located beside the Martin Goodman Trail, Sunnyside pool has been around for over 90 years. It's the largest outdoor pool in the city. There's a nice playground and also a wading pool right near this location. Many people flock here during the summer for a picnic and a swim. Of course, it's only open in summer.

307 ALEXANDRA PARK POOL

275 Bathurst St
Downtown ①
toronto.ca

Alexandra Park is a nice outdoor pool. It's also a great spot to catch a glimpse of the CN Tower. The pool is located right beside a playground, and there's a bike path nearby. It's not a fancy pool; there are no slides. It is open late, usually until 8 pm.

308 HANLAN'S POINT BEACH
AT: TORONTO ISLANDS
Downtown ②
torontoisland.com/
hanlans.php

Hanlan's Point Beach used to be a resort during the early 1900s. The area is much quieter now. Hanlan's Point has several facilities that include baseball diamonds and a clothing-optional beach area. The view from the beach is amazing during sunset, as it faces west.

309 CHERRY BEACH
End of Cherry St
Downtown ②
toronto.ca

Cherry Beach is very popular and can get crowded. But if you travel further along the beach to the area near the windsurfing club, it gets much quieter, and it's a nice spot to soak up some sunlight. The beach is not a part of the main strip so you won't find any food vendors, but you'll have it all to yourself.

310 BLUFFER'S PARK BEACH
1 Brimley Road S
Scarborough ⑦
ON M1M 3W3
toronto.ca

Located on the east side of the GTA, Bluffer's beach is the nicest swimming spot in Toronto. The man-made beach sits at the base of the Scarborough Bluffs. These cliffs are stunning; they're tall white limestone bluffs that reflect the sunlight. Everyone comes here for engagement and wedding photos.

5 accessible places to
PHOTOGRAPH THE TORONTO SKYLINE

311 CALEDON MOUNTAIN

Highpoint Side Road
Caledon ⑪
VWMM+XG

A short drive up Highway 10 into Caledon will reward you with stunning views of the Great Lakes lowlands and the GTA. On a clear day, you can see for kilometres. It's also fun to drive around this area and try to guess which mansion belongs to Elton John.

312 RIVERDALE PARK

550 Broadview Ave
East End ⑤
toronto.ca

Riverdale is located in the Don Valley. There are baseball diamonds, an outdoor pool and lots of great spots for picnicking. The park is divided into two parts, east and west. You can access both by a footbridge that crosses the Don Valley Parkway. At sunset, the CN Tower glows with pink light.

313 HUMBER BAY PARK EAST

Martin Goodman
Trail
Etobicoke ⑧
ON M8V 3W9
toronto.ca

If you visit Humber Bay, your view of the skyline will look across the water to the CN Tower and the Harbourfront neighbourhood. You'll be able to see the high-rise condos and buildings of the Financial District all scattered behind the CN Tower.

314 **POLSON PIER**

11 Polson St
Downtown ②
polsonpier.com

If you wander up and down Polson Pier, you'll find you can catch lots of great glimpses of the skyline. In my opinion, the view from Polson is at its best just as the sky starts to turn dark. The lights from the Financial District are pretty.

315 **IRELAND PARK**

Queen's Quay W
Downtown ②
irelandpark
foundation.com

You can take some pretty dramatic photos from this location. Ireland Park is the site of several sculptures dedicated to the Irish immigrants who came to Canada during the Potato Famine. It's possible to capture the sculptures and the Toronto skyline in the same photograph.

313 **TORONTO SKYLINE FROM HUMBER BAY PARK EAST**

5 beautiful
GARDENS in the GTA

316 **TORONTO MUSIC GARDEN**
479 Queens Quay W
Downtown ②
*harbourfront
centre.com/venues/
torontomusicgarden*

Toronto Music Garden is a pretty spot right near the marina. There's a fun spiral garden full of plants. Little kids love to run around this structure looking for the sculpture at the centre. There's also a nice set of steps under some weeping willow trees where you can make yourself comfortable.

317 **ALLAN GARDENS**
160 Gerrard St E
Downtown ①
*toronto.ca/allan-
gardens-conservatory*

The park is very nice, but it's the 100-year-old Edwardian conservatory that's the highlight. The staff try to rotate displays to match the seasons and holidays. Entry is free, and it's open until 5 pm daily. Inside, it feels like a scene from a fantasy novel.

318 **KEW GARDENS**
2075 Queen St E
East End ⑤
toronto.ca

Kew Gardens is a large and busy park near the lakeshore. The Martin Goodman Trail runs along the waterfront. The children's garden must be booked in advance but your little ones will love it. There's also a large play structure. A vast open area hosts performances from the Beaches Jazz Festival each year.

319 BAMBOO FOREST

AT: UNIVERSITY
OF TORONTO

160 College St
Downtown ①

The Bamboo Forest is a serene green space located in the Terrence Donnelly Centre on the University of Toronto campus. It's a quiet space where you'll find students studying on benches. Sometimes couples come here for an afternoon of peace and togetherness on a bench.

320 EDWARDS GARDENS

755 Lawrence Ave E
North York ④
torontobotanical
garden.ca

Edwards Gardens are about water. There's a very pretty pond here with a small waterfall and a cute bridge. You'll find a lot of pathways lined with garden beds. Many locals will book the location for their wedding. The nearby Toronto Botanical Garden is a nice bonus to this site.

316 TORONTO MUSIC GARDEN

5 spooky
HALLOWEEN HAUNTS

---

321 HALLOWEEN HAUNT
AT: CANADA'S WONDERLAND

1 Canada's
Wonderland Drive
Vaughan ⑪
ON L6A 1S6
+1 905 832 8131
*canadaswonderland.
com/play/haunt*

Every year Canada's Wonderland sets up a haunted house experience inside the amusement park. Locals flock to the event. It's scary! The park stays open after regular hours on October weekends. Some of the rides are open, and as you wander through, zombies might chase you.

322 MARTINO MANOR

7 Mackintosh Ave
Etobicoke ⑧
ON M8Y 3C8
+1 647 802 5045
martinomanor.com

Martino Manor is located behind an Italian restaurant. It opens at the beginning of October every year. This haunted house is one of those quirky places that you won't find unless you really dig into local culture. Entry is 20 dollar and it's worth the expense. Before visiting, head in to Mamma Martino's for a classic Italian dinner.

323 HAUNTED HIGH PARK
AT: COLBORNE LODGE,
HIGH PARK

11 Colborne Lodge Dr
West End ⑥
+1 416 923 1171
highpark.org

High Park hosts a haunted house event. It's fairly family-friendly: kids 10 and over will enjoy the stories. Park staff share spooky legends about an event that took place at High Park. The storytelling takes place at Colborne Lodge, and it's recommended that you reserve tickets.

324 NIGHT OF DREAD
AT: DUFFERIN
GROVE PARK

875 Dufferin St
West End ⑥
clayandpaper
theatre.org/our-work/
night-of-dread

The Clay and Paper Theatre has been hosting *The Night of Dread* for 20 years now. On a Saturday evening close to Halloween, participants meet in Dufferin Grove park wearing masks and costumes. They then proceed through the park in a kind of parade, which includes sparklers and a lot of pageantry. Afterwards, parade goers can join in a variety of other activities, like a bonfire, for some great community engagement.

325 LEGENDS OF HORROR
AT: CASA LOMA

1 Austin Terrace
Midtown ③
legendsofhorror.ca

Casa Loma is a major tourist stop, but visiting it during October for Legends of Horror is a different experience. You get to access the tunnels and other buildings not always available during regular public tours. It's creepy walking through those underground passages at night. The tour is an hour long.

The 5 most popular
S P O R T S   T E A M S *to watch*

---

326 TORONTO RAPTORS / BASKETBALL
AT: SCOTIABANK ARENA
40 Bay St
Downtown ②
nba.com/raptors

"We the North", has become a common saying here in Toronto. In 2019 the Raptors were named NBA Champions for the first time in the team's history. Toronto has embraced the Raptors, and the vibe is very positive. Drake makes regular appearances at games. You'll see him courtside.

327 TORONTO MAPLE LEAFS / HOCKEY
AT: SCOTIABANK ARENA
40 Bay St
Downtown ②
nhl.com/mapleleafs

Attending a Leafs game is expensive. If you do go, you will be a part of something linked to the identity of many Canadians. In the past families have crowded around the TV to watch *Hockey Night* in Canada.

328 HAMILTON TIGER-CATS / AMERICAN FOOTBALL
AT: TIM HORTONS FIELD
64 Melrose Avenue N
Hamilton ⑨
ON L8L 8C1
ticats.ca

Canada has a proud football tradition. The lesser-known CFL (Canadian Football League) hosts a series of Canadian professional football teams. While the league doesn't garner as much attention as the NFL, games are still exciting. The venues and crowds are much smaller, so it's a more intimate experience.

329 TORONTO BLUE JAYS / BASEBALL
AT: ROGERS CENTRE

1 Blue Jays Way
Downtown ②
mlb.com/bluejays

The Blue Jays are another long-standing team in Toronto. The Rogers Centre (originally named SkyDome) is a pretty interesting building. The roof is retractable, so some games will be open air. It's fun to sit in the lower seats but the view from the 500s is spectacular and cheap.

330 TORONTO FC / SOCCER
AT: BMO FIELD

170 Princes' Blvd
Downtown ②
torontofc.ca

Toronto FC is a relatively new team in the city. Hockey is no longer the only sport in town, as soccer is quickly gaining in popularity. Games are played at BMO Field, a beautiful open-air venue located in Exhibition Place. You can get great seats quite easily.

329 ROGERS CENTRE / TORONTO BLUE JAYS

5

KITSCHY PLACES

in Toronto

---

331 BARBERIAN'S STEAKHOUSE

7 Elm St
Downtown ①
+1 416 597 0335
barberians.com

If you're in for a blast from the past, you'll love the classic red-and-white wallpaper and lantern-style light fixtures at this classic steakhouse. The dining room must look very similar to the way it did when the restaurant opened in 1959.

332 TED'S RESTAURANT

404 Old Kingston Rd
Scarborough ⑦
ON M1C 1B6
+1 416 282 2204

Ted's Restaurant is a real mom-and-pop operation that serves classic greasy spoon food, making it a great place to have a traditional Ontario community diner experience. The decor hasn't changed in ages, but they have added some very fun decorative vignettes throughout the restaurant.

333 TCHOTCHKE HOUSE

37 Bertmount Ave
East End ⑤

The name says it all. This house is chock-full of *tchotchke* dolls. Even the entire exterior is decorated with dolls, making it a real neighbourhood landmark. While Leslieville is fairly quiet, and most houses have well-kept gardens, the Tchotchke House is quite a sight to behold.

334 SWAN DIVE

1631 Dundas St W
West End ⑥
+1 647 347 0099

Swan Dive is a fun, vibrant bar on Dundas West with a quirky and very eclectic decor. They are all about having a good time: you can even buy sunglasses and bottles of bubbles for added entertainment. The bar is decorated with vintage photographs that have been sealed onto the countertop of the bar.

335 SHAMEFUL TIKI ROOM

1378 Queen St W
West End ⑥
shamefultikiroom.com/
toronto

Walking into this place feels like you've entered the movie set of a *National Lampoon* movie or stepped back into a 1950s tiki bar. The tropical decor takes kitsch to a new level, with bamboo everywhere. Even the tasty cocktails are retro.

5 MOVIES and the LOCATIONS where they were filmed in Toronto

336 A CHRISTMAS STORY

Cherry St at
the Portlands
Downtown ②
youtube.com/watch?
v=UwvEBhTYV5c

This is a classic North American Christmas movie. Each year families watch it and reminisce about Christmas in the 1940s. The famous "Oh Fudge!" scene was filmed in the Portlands. You can drive down the same road singing Christmas carols to commemorate the moment, if you wish.

337 THE SHAPE OF WATER

Keating Channel,
Lake Shore Blvd
East, just south of
Corktown Common
Downtown ②

This is a dark romance film by director Guillermo del Toro. Toronto has appeared in many of Del Toro's movies. *The Shape of Water* was filmed all over Toronto, but the final climax of the plot was filmed at Keating Channel in the docklands area.

338 RESIDENT EVIL: AFTERLIFE

TORONTO CITY HALL
100 Queen St W
Downtown ①

The film uses multiple locations throughout Toronto as part of the movie set. In the movie, Toronto City Hall is turned into a post-apocalyptic location. Milla Jovovich flies her spaceship over city hall and lands dramatically amidst the ruins.

339 THE INCREDIBLE HULK (2008)
KNOX COLLEGE, UNIVERSITY OF TORONTO

59 St. George St
Downtown ①
youtube.com/watch?
v=eQC7flDRhJo

This film used multiple locations throughout the university campus, but one of the most notable scenes was shot at Knox College. The Hulk smashes through the campus in an action-packed fight scene and ruins a bunch of military vehicles.

340 CHICAGO
DANFORTH MUSIC HALL

147 Danforth Avenue
East End ⑤

It bothers many movie fans that the entirety of the film *Chicago* was shot in Toronto. The movie takes advantage of stately buildings like Osgoode Hall and the Danforth Music Hall, to add a historical feel to the movie.

YONGE-DUNDAS SQUARE

50 PLACES
FOR CULTURE

5 *fun* **FESTIVALS**
throughout summer and fall

---

341 **PRIDE TORONTO**
VARIOUS VENUES
Downtown
pridetoronto.com

Pride is huge in Toronto. The whole city gears up for the event. There are advertisements for specials, hip happenings, etc. The festival involves an opening ceremony, some smaller more intimate occurrences, a bunch of fun parties and one huge parade to cap off the celebration. It's a month-long affair worth visiting.

342 **JUNCTION NIGHT MARKET**
AT: JUNCTION TRAIN PLATFORM
2960 Dundas St W
West End ⑥
junctionmarket.ca/
night-market

The Junction Night Market is a one-night event held in July. It is a part of the regular Junction Farmers Market but with food, music and lots more. Local vendors and breweries provide samples. Food tickets are reasonably priced, and all proceeds go to charity.

343 JUST FOR LAUGHS
VARIOUS VENUES
jfl42.com

Everyone knows about the Just For Laughs comedy festival in Montreal, but Toronto also hosts events. It's a huge festival featuring comics from around the world. Several venues will host different comedy events. It's best to check the website. Some folks will visit Montreal for the summer edition and Toronto in fall.

344 RIBFEST
AT: CENTENNIAL PARK
256 Centennial Park Road Etobicoke ⑧ **ON M9C 5N3**
torontoribfest.com

Ribfest is huge. It's much more than ribs. There's a pretty decent midway, live music, and all sorts of different vendors offering everything from henna tattoos to funky T-shirts. Ribfest is run by the local Rotary Club and is used to raise funds for community projects.

345 SALSA ON ST. CLAIR
Saint Clair Ave W from Winona Drive to Christie St Midtown ③
salsaintoronto.com/ lineup/salsa-on-st-clair

Salsa on St. Clair celebrates everything Latin you can find in Toronto. There are free dancing lessons and lots of vendors selling Latin foods. The event also organizes a variety of art exhibitions in different locations. At times the entire street will be filled with people dancing.

The 5 best small venues for seeing
LIVE THEATRE

―――――――

346 TARRAGON THEATRE
30 Bridgeman Ave
Midtown ③
+1 416 531 1827
tarragontheatre.com

Tarragon is one of those smaller theatres where you're going to see a lot of work you won't find on the mainstream stages. They present new pieces as well as older plays from both Canadian and international playwrights. They offer a selection of courses to help you write your first play or direct your first performance.

347 FACTORY THEATRE
125 Bathurst St
Downtown ①
+1 416 504 9971
factorytheatre.ca

Factory's mandate is to provide Canadian artists with a venue that supports their work. The theatre shows exclusively Canadian plays. They also help artists develop their skills as actors and playwrights. You'll find lots of variety in this theatre and reasonably priced tickets.

348 YOUNG PEOPLE'S THEATRE

165 Front St E
Downtown ①
+1 416 862 2222
youngpeoplestheatre.ca

School children in Toronto know this theatre well. They provide high-quality performances for children ranging in age from toddler to teenager. Performances go from musical productions to serious dramas about issues Canadian teens are facing. St. Lawrence Market is next door, so go for lunch after a performance.

349 COAL MINE THEATRE

1454 Danforth Ave
East End ⑤
+1 800 838 3006
coalminetheatre.com

This is a pretty cool theatre. It only has 80 seats. Performances are intimate. They call themselves the Off-Off-Broadway Theatre. You'll find experienced veterans with big names working alongside brand-new actors still learning the ropes. They showcase plays that are edgy and controversial. No fluff here.

350 BERKELEY STREET THEATRE

26 Berkeley St
Downtown ①
+1 416 368 3110
canadianstage.com

Berkeley Street is another small and intimate venue. This not-for-profit theatre provides Canadian Stage – a contemporary performing arts organization – with another location that supports its growth and development. Canadian Stage offers workshops and provides a venue for Canadian actors and playwrights to develop their skills.

5 places where you can learn about
CANADIAN HISTORY

---

351 **FORT YORK**
250 Fort York Blvd
Downtown ②
+1 416 392 6907
toronto.ca/explore-
enjoy/fort-york-
national-historic-site

Fort York is a big site. They do daily re-enactments of military life in Toronto during the war of 1812. There's a large gallery here where you can learn how Canadians defended themselves from the American invasion. Fort York also hosts an array of community events, so it's about more than history.

351 FORT YORK

352 CAMPBELL HOUSE MUSEUM

160 Queen St W
Downtown ①
+1 416 597 0227
campbellhouse
museum.ca

This is just one of several cool little museums located throughout the city. The space houses a small collection of artifacts associated with the life of Chief Justice William Campbell. The museum also provides a wide range of informative programming like tours and travelling exhibits.

353 MACKENZIE HOUSE

82 Bond St
Downtown ①
+1 416 392 6915
toronto.ca/
mackenzie-house

This is the former home of the first Mayor of Toronto, William Lyon Mackenzie. Visitors will gain insight into Victorian life here in Toronto. The museum operates a working recreated print shop, which is pretty cool. Much of the history is interpreted through the writings of Mackenzie himself.

354 TORONTO NECROPOLIS CEMETERY

200 Winchester St
Downtown ①

It may seem morbid, but visiting this cemetery will give you a good idea of Canadian history. William Lyon Mackenzie is buried here, along with other notable Canadian figures. The architecture is Gothic and there are incredible vistas from several locations within the grounds.

355 SCARBOROUGH MUSEUM

1007 Brimley Road
Scarborough ⑦
ON M1P 3E8
+1 416 338 8807
toronto.ca/
scarborough-museum

The focus of this museum is to educate about local rural life from the 1850s to the early 1900s. This property has some beautiful walking trails. Several historical buildings have also been moved to this site.

The 5 largest
MUSIC FESTIVALS
in Toronto

---

356 VELD MUSIC FESTIVAL

AT: DOWNSVIEW PARK
**1-35 Carl Hall Road
North York** ⑪
veldmusicfestival.com

This is a two-day festival taking place on the first weekend of August. It's big, loud and chaotic. If you like electronic dance music this is the event to visit. The festival attracts about 70.000 people for a night of high-energy dancing. Bring water; they often run out.

357 TD TORONTO JAZZ FESTIVAL

VARIOUS VENUES
torontojazz.com

This well-known jazz festival brings some of the biggest names in jazz to Toronto. Performances range from concerts in large venues to small intimate events held in local parks. The event lasts for ten days, and there's something for every music lover to enjoy.

358 NXNE – NORTH BY NORTHEAST FESTIVAL
VARIOUS VENUES
+1 416 901 6963
nxne.com

North by Northeast is a music and gaming festival lasting for seven days in June. The festival highlights new music. The idea is to promote Canadian and international up-and-coming musicians. The gaming portion is interesting as well, with many live gaming competitions. Purchasing a wristband gets you early access to shows.

359 CANADIAN MUSIC WEEK
VARIOUS VENUES
+1 905 858 4747
cmw.net/music

Canadian Music Week is all about showcasing Canadian talent. For one week, the city hosts a huge selection of Canadian artists at different locations. There's also a conference for Canadian music professionals to attend. Taking place in May, it's a chance to see often-overlooked Canadian talent.

360 HILLSIDE FESTIVAL
AT: GUELPH LAKE CONSERVATION AREA
7743 Conservation Rd Guelph ⑨
ON N1H 6J1
+1 519 763 6396
hillsidefestival.ca

Located in Guelph, this event is a short drive out of the city, but it's worth the trip. Held annually in July, this festival is family-friendly. There is camping on-site, but it fills up fast, so book early. The festival's mission is to promote creativity, self-expression and environmental awareness.

5 *places to find*

FREE *or* ALMOST FREE PERFORMANCES

---

361 SHAKESPEARE IN HIGH PARK

AT: HIGH PARK AMPHITHEATRE

200 Parkside Drive West End ⑥

canadianstage.com

Every summer, the graceful words of Shakespeare fill the amphitheatre at High Park. Pay what you can to enter, or donate 25 dollar to reserve yourself a cushioned seat. Bring some food and enjoy a picnic while you are treated to a performance that features both drama students and professional actors.

362 LIVE ON THE PATIO

AT: ROY THOMSON HALL

60 Simcoe St Downtown ①

+1 416 872 4255

roythomsonhall.com/ live-on-the-patio

Twice a week during July and August, live performances are hosted on the patio at Roy Thomson Hall. This beautiful venue hosts a mixed line-up of Canadian bands. It's an opportunity to sit, enjoy a drink and watch the amazing hidden talents of Canada. Admission is free. Come early to get a seat; chairs are limited.

363 TORONTO OUTDOOR PICTURE SHOW

VARIOUS LOCATIONS

topictureshow.com

Throughout the summer, TOPS shows family-friendly films that follow a theme. The screenings are free, check the website for times and dates. Bring blankets or a lawn chair and snacks. Showings start at 8 pm, right around dusk. Films range from Disney to Charlie Chaplin.

364 CANADIAN OPERA COMPANY

AT: FOUR SEASONS CENTRE FOR THE PERFORMING ARTS
145 Queen St W
Downtown ①
+1 416 363 8231
coc.ca

This is a unique experience. Even if you don't like opera, go! They offer more than just opera performances. The venue is beautiful: you can enjoy talented musicians while sitting in a large open space with views over the streets of Toronto. Look at some pictures online to see why it comes highly recommended.

365 CHEVY MUSIC INDIE FRIDAYS

AT: YONGE-DUNDAS SQUARE
1 Dundas St E
Downtown ①
ydsquare.ca/
indiefridays

Sponsored by Chevrolet, Indie Fridays provides free concerts highlighting a huge variety of Canadian musicians from all music genres. Wander down to the square, catch a free concert, then take full advantage of all the delicious food vendors nearby. It's a good spot to start an evening out.

364 CANADIAN OPERA COMPANY

The 5 most comprehensive
ART GALLERIES *that are*
NOT *the* AGO

---

366 **ART MUSEUM**
AT: UNIVERSITY
OF TORONTO
7 Hart House Circle,
15 King's College
Circle
Downtown ①
+1 416 978 8398
artmuseum.utoronto.ca

The art museum comprises two buildings located side by side: the Justina M. Barnicke Gallery and the University of Toronto Art Centre. The large venue hosts an array of exhibitions as well as events. The Hart House has established a very extensive collection of Canadian art, representing a wide range of artists.

369 **THE POWER PLANT**

367 BAU-XI GALLERY

340 Dundas St W
Downtown ①
+1 416 977 0600
bau-xi.com

Bau-Xi is a small and intimate, commercially run gallery. It's across the street from the AGO. They represent a mix of contemporary artists, many of whom are based in Toronto. The staff are friendly and happy to answer any questions you may have about the current exhibit.

368 COOPER COLE

1134 Dupont St
Midtown ③
+1 416 531 8000
coopercolegallery.com

Cooper Cole is a small independent gallery. It's intimate and very exclusive. They are not always open, so it's best to call ahead and make an appointment to visit. One of the advantages is that you'll get a lot of attention as you stroll through this high-end art space.

369 THE POWER PLANT

AT: HARBOURFRONT CENTRE
231 Queens Quay W
Downtown ②
+1 416 973 4949
thepowerplant.org

The Power Plant is a large public gallery in the centre of the Harbourfront neighbourhood. It's easy to visit some of the other venues located nearby as well. There's always something really interesting happening here. They have a good schedule of events that will appeal to all sorts of people. Admission is free.

370 MCMICHAEL GALLERY

10365 Islington Ave
Kleinburg ⑪
ON L0J 1C0
+1 905 893 1121
mcmichael.com

You'll need to head out of town to visit, so make it a day trip. The gallery has an extensive collection of Canadian painters, including the very famous Group of Seven. Visit earlier in the morning or after 2 pm as the gallery can be full of school groups at midday.

5 places or events that highlight
TORONTO'S DIVERSITY

---

371 **AGA KHAN MUSEUM**
77 Wynford Drive
North York ④
+1 416 646 4677
agakhanmuseum.org

The Aga Khan works to promote understanding of Islamic culture and religion. The museum and the grounds are nicely kept, and they host a variety of interesting exhibits. They also conduct workshops and courses that anyone can attend.

372 **CARIBANA TORONTO**
Exhibition Place to
Lake Shore
Boulevard ending at
Saskatchewan Road
Downtown ②
+1 416 391 5608
caribanatoronto.com,
torontocarnival.com

Still called 'Caribana' by locals, the Toronto Caribbean Carnival is a 4-week celebration of culture and inclusivity. The highlight of the Carnival is the parade, which takes place during the August long weekend. The parade and costumes rival those found at the Carnival in Rio. You can purchase tickets to the opening ceremony or enjoy the parade for free as it moves through the streets.

373 SMALL WORLD MUSIC FESTIVAL

180 Shaw St,
Studio 101
Downtown ①
+1 416 536 5439
smallworldmusic.com

Occurring yearly in September, the Small World Music Festival sees international and Canadian bands take the stage to highlight music from all over the globe. Many of the performances at Small World Music Centre are free. The festival highlights traditional music as well as international contemporary artists.

374 SARAH AND CHAIM NEUBERGER HOLOCAUST EDUCATION CENTRE

4600 Bathurst St,
4th Floor
North York ⑪
+1 416 631 5689
holocaustcentre.com

The museum in the Lipa Green Centre at Sherman Campus is a small but extremely interesting place. They offer a selection of programs that work to educate the public – adults as well as children – about the Holocaust. It has been internationally recognized for its efforts. If you want to visit, please call ahead, as they don't generally have hours where the public can wander through.

375 TD MOSAIC SOUTH ASIAN FESTIVAL OF MISSISSAUGA

300 City Centre Dr
Mississauga ⑧
ON L5B 3C1
+1 416 388 9596
mosaicfest.com

Mississauga and Brampton are hotbeds for South Asian culture in the GTA. The TD Mosaic Festival highlights all cultures from South Asia. There are family activities as well as concerts at Celebration Square that run late into the evening. Many local bands and South Asian cultural groups will perform throughout the weekend.

5 *fun*
FILM FESTIVALS
in Toronto

---

376 TORONTO INTERNATIONAL FILM FESTIVAL
AT: TIFF BELL LIGHTBOX
350 King Street West
Downtown ①
tiff.net

TIFF is a giant, internationally recognized film festival that rivals the Cannes film festival. Many famous filmmakers began their careers with showings at TIFF. Hollywood celebrities flock to Toronto for exclusive viewings. The public can also purchase tickets to see these up-and-coming films.

377 PENDANCE FILM FESTIVAL
AT: TIFF BELL LIGHTBOX
350 King St W
Downtown ①
pendancefilmfestival.ca

Pendance is an intense festival. The organizers are meticulous in the films they select, showing the best of Canadian and international films. The festival is quite new; 2020 will be its third year of operations. It's quickly gaining a fantastic reputation and you'll find you can still obtain tickets with ease.

378 TORONTO INDEPENDENT FILM FESTIVAL

AT: CARLTON CINEMA
**20 Carlton Street
Downtown** ①
*torontoshort.com/
toindie*

It's easy to confuse this festival with TIFF, they are however two separate events. This one is a marathon festival that occurs in September each year. All the films are independently created. Tickets are reasonably priced, and you can watch a collection of short films or a longer-length feature.

379 TORONTO QUEER FILM FESTIVAL

VARIOUS LOCATIONS
*torontoqueerfilm
fest.com*

Organized by a collective of artists and filmmakers, the goal was to create a festival that celebrated films focusing on queer and trans culture. The festival takes place at different venues through-out the city and tickets can be purchased online. The tickets are priced on a sliding scale, between 5 and 15 dollar, so that the event is accessible to all regardless of your budget.

380 IMAGINENATIVE

VARIOUS LOCATIONS
+1 416 585 2333
imaginenative.org

This is the largest festival celebrating films by indigenous peoples in the world. It is run entirely by local indigenous groups in Ontario. The festival seeks to promote ideas of environmental sustainability and to present films which accurately depict the lives of these cultural groups, both in Canada and abroad.

The 5 **PAINTINGS** at the **AGO** that most locals pick as their favourite

---

Art Gallery of Ontario
317 Dundas St W
Downtown ①
+1 416 979 6648
ago.ca

381 **SPIRIT BEAR POSSESSING A MAN'S SOUL**
BY DAVID RUBEN PIQTOUKUN
Gallery 106
Walker Court,
Floor Vitrine

The AGO has a very impressive collection of the world-famous carvings of the Inuit of Canada. This particular sculpture is made of stone and ivory. The detail on the ivory man is incredible for its size.

382 **LA SOUPE**
BY PABLO PICASSO
Gallery 137
Margaret Eaton
Gallery

Picasso is such a famous name in art and the AGO proudly displays their piece. The blues of the background and the dresses are calming and quite beautiful. You will find both Canadian and international artists at the AGO.

383 SOLDIER AND GIRL AT THE STATION
BY ALEX COLVILLE
Gallery 206
Thomson Canadian

Colville is from Canada's East Coast. His style can be described as surreal. Each painting seems mundane, but there's more to his work than meets the eye. His wife is found in many of his pieces. Some say that after her death, Colville lost all of his inspiration.

384 THUNDERBIRD
BY EMILY CARR
Gallery 217
Thomson Canadian

Emily Carr is another Canadian art icon. Heritage Canada has created short videos teaching Canadians about her contributions to our culture and heritage. Her paintings only gained significance after her passing in 1945. Her work often depicted the totem poles in British Columbia.

385 THE WEST WIND
BY TOM THOMSON
Gallery 126
Richard Barry
Fudger Rotunda

Thomson is another member of the Group of Seven. This is one of my favourite paintings in the AGO. It depicts a lone pine tree set against the wilderness of Algonquin Park. Many people make the trek to the park to view the pine tree that inspired the painting. Be aware that there is some debate as to whether the site is actually correct.

5 great
COMEDY CLUBS

386 **THE SECOND CITY**
  51 Mercer St
  Downtown ①
  +1 416 343 0011
  secondcity.com

Second City has been a kickstarter for the careers of many famous Canadian comedians. Some notable names are Eugene Levy *(American Pie)* and John Candy *(Plains, Trains and Automobiles)*. Second City will be moving to a new location at York Street at the end of 2020.

387 **COMEDY BAR**
  945 Bloor St W
  Midtown ③
  +1 416 551 6540
  comedybar.ca

There aren't many comedy bars in Toronto, but this one is very popular. They offer stand-up, improv and a selection of other shows. You can also sign up for one of their workshops. They pride themselves on offering independent comedy. You won't find any Yuk Yuk's performers here.

388 **ABSOLUTE COMEDY**
  2335 Yonge St
  Uptown ③
  +1 416 486 7700
  absolutecomedy.ca/
  toronto

Absolute Comedy has an affordable dinner & show combination. The dinners are good basic plates, and the comedians are pretty funny. They partner with organizations like Just for Laughs and Yuk Yuk's to offer comedy workshops.

389 THE RIVOLI

332 Queen St W
Downtown ①
Pool Hall:
+1 416 596 1501
Dining Area:
+1 416 596 1908
rivoli.ca

The Rivoli often hosts an array of comedic performances. It's a restaurant, concert venue and pool hall. The food is good, and it can surprise you. Call ahead on weekends for reservations. It's not what you would expect of a place that hosts both concerts and pool tournaments.

390 THE CORNER COMEDY CLUB

946 Queen St E
East End ⑤
*thecornercomedy.com/
toronto-east*

The Corner Comedy Club has two locations in Toronto. This one is a little smaller and more intimate than the location on John Street. They serve drinks, and everything else is fairly bare-bones, but the comedians are very talented.

GRANGE PARK

20 THINGS TO DO WITH CHILDREN

5 PARKS
your kids will love visiting

---

391 MARIE CURTIS PARK

2 Forty Second St
Etobicoke ⑧
ON M8W 3P2
toronto.ca

Marie Curtis Park is situated in the far southwest corner of Toronto along the lakeshore. It connects to many of the lakefront trails, and is a good place to bring the family for a picnic. There's a splash pad and a beach here. The willow trees and winding paths are beautiful.

392 DUFFERIN GROVE PARK

875 Dufferin Park
Avenue
West End ⑥
dufferinpark.ca

Dufferin Grove is a large park featuring all the classic park elements like a wading pool. They also have two very cool wood-fired pizza ovens. On certain days you can bring your handmade pizza over, and they will cook it for you for a small fee. Fun!

393 KEW GARDENS

2075 Queen St E
East End ⑤
toronto.ca

Everyone knows about Kew Gardens, and with good reason. The Kew Children's Garden is amazing. There's a canopy walk as well as cool trampolines set into the ground. The kitchen garden makes for a delightful stroll. In winter you can skate on the outdoor rink.

394 CORKTOWN COMMON

155 Bayview Avenue
Downtown ①
toronto.ca

The playground here is a cool spot for kids. It was designed using elements from nature to create unique slides and swings. There's also a splash pad, and if you wander along some of the paths, you'll find a wetland that connects to the Don River. Look for frogs and turtles here.

395 GRANGE PARK

Between Beverly St
and McCaul St
Downtown ①
grangeparktoronto.ca

Grange Park offers a lot for families. It has a splash pad and climber, plus mature trees for shade on a hot summer day. There's a leash-free zone for dogs, as well. You can enjoy a nice view of the CN Tower and the architecture of the AGO here.

395 GRANGE PARK

5 fun places to see
ANIMALS

---

396 AFRICAN LION SAFARI

1386 Cooper Road
Hamilton ⑨
+1 519 623 2620
lionsafari.com

African Lion Safari is designed to make you feel like you are wandering through an African landscape. The park allows you to drive your car through the grounds. Animals are not in cages, they run free. You can also hop on their safari busses or take a boat cruise. The lion safari is open for visitors from April to October.

397 CAMBRIDGE BUTTERFLY CONSERVATORY

2500 Kossuth Road
Cambridge ⑨
ON N3H 4R7
+1 519 653 1234
cambridgebutterfly.com

A bit of a drive from the heart of Toronto, you can combine this site with other nearby venues to create a full day. They offer children's programming, or you can wander through the Cambridge Butterfly Conservatory on your own. You are almost guaranteed to have the butterflies land on you.

398 FAR ENOUGH FARM

Centre Island
Downtown ②
centreisland.ca/
far-enough-farm

On Centre Island, you will find a fun petting zoo. They have all kinds of farm animals. Most are rarer breeds. My personal favourite is the pot-bellied pigs, adorable and weird at the same time. The Centreville amusement park is right next door, so you can plan a full day visit here. Please check the website before visiting during the spring and fall months as the farm closes during the winter.

399 REPTILIA ZOO

2501 Rutherford Rd
Vaughan ⑪
ON L4K 2N6
+1 905 761 6223
reptilia.org

Reptilia Zoo will soon have two locations in the GTA. The large indoor space houses a huge variety of reptiles. You can see crocodiles and pythons. During their shows, they offer visitors the opportunity to get up close and personal with the animals.

400 HIGH PARK ZOO
AT: HIGH PARK

Deer Pen Road
West End ⑥
highparktoronto.com/
zoo.php

High Park Zoo is free to visit. It has been in High Park for 125 years. They have some fun programs in which kids can feed the llamas or pet baby chicks. The walk to the park can be a lot for little legs, bring a stroller. Unlike many of the other small zoos in the area, High Park is open all year round.

The best 5
TOBOGGANING HILLS
for any age in **T O**

---

401 **CHRISTIE PITS PARK**
750 Bloor St W
Midtown ③
toronto.ca

Christie Pits Park has several good hills for tobogganing. The advantage is that there are lots of different slopes in different sizes. There is a suitable one for every age. It can get busy, however. If the crowds are too much to handle here, go to Bickford Park. It also has a good hill and it is within walking distance.

#05- TRINITY BELLWOODS PARK

402 **WITHROW PARK**

725 Logan Avenue
East End ⑤
toronto.ca

Withrow Park is located in the East End, and is another popular spot. What's good about this hill are the steps built into the side of it, which can be helpful when everything gets icy. The hill itself is pretty long, so you'll get a decent run here.

403 **LINUS PARK**

125 Seneca Hill Drive
North York ⑪
toronto.ca

This park in the north end, also known as Crestview Park, is very popular with families. It's a long hill with a gentler slope, good for little ones. They've also installed lights so you can go night tobogganing here.

404 **LITHUANIA PARK**

155 Oakmount Road
West End ⑥
toronto.ca

This is a hill for thrill-seekers. It's steep, and the run is fast. The good news is that the bottom of the hill provides lots of slow-down space, so you won't end up on the street or in the bushes.

405 **TRINITY BELLWOODS PARK**

790 Queen St W
Downtown ①
trinitybellwoods.ca

Trinity Bellwoods is a large park with several good hills. You'll find families here who might have a large range of ages – there is something for the youngest kids as well as for the older ones. One of the most popular hills is in the leash-free dog area.

5 places to take kids on
RAINY DAYS

---

406 RIPLEY'S AQUARIUM
288 Bremner Blvd
Downtown ②
+1 647 351 3474
ripleyaquariums.com/
canada

Ripley's Aquarium is big, busy and filled with some pretty cool underwater exhibits. It will be packed on weekends, so it's best to visit early or go during the week. However, on weekdays from September to June you'll encounter large numbers of school groups visiting the aquarium. Most groups will be leaving by about 1.30 pm, so visiting later in the day is best.

407 FANTASY FAIR
AT: WOODBINE MALL
500 Rexdale Blvd
Etobicoke ⑧
ON M9W 6K5
+1 416 674 8684
fantasyfair.ca/rides-
and-attraction

This is a pretty cool spot. You don't expect a mall in Etobicoke to house such a large indoor amusement park. It's the largest in Ontario. The park has bumper cars, a Ferris wheel, a small train and several other rides to keep the kids busy on a rainy day.

408 ROYAL ONTARIO MUSEUM

100 Queens Park
Downtown ①
+1 416 586 8000
rom.on.ca/en/whats-on/all-programs/kids

The ROM is a popular destination in Toronto. It can get busy, so plan accordingly. My personal favourite with kids is the floor that houses the full suits of armour. Kids, especially boys, tend to be awed by these massive metal outfits. They have some great children's programming, check the website.

409 CINESPHERE

AT: ONTARIO PLACE
955 Lake Shore
Boulevard W
Downtown ②
+1 416 314 9938
ontarioplace.com/en/cinesphere

Located inside Ontario Place, the Cinesphere offers a variety of movies on their IMAX screen. Some are short flicks designed for IMAX, others are mainstream Hollywood movies adapted to the screen. Either way, the popcorn is fresh, and the tickets are reasonably priced.

410 BATA SHOE MUSEUM

327 Bloor St W
Midtown ③
+1 416 979 7799
batashoemuseum.ca/family-fun

This is a funky little museum that's fairly well known in Toronto. They usually host some fun children's activities on weekends. It won't be as busy as other locations in the city, so your kids might get to experience the exhibits a little more than in other spots.

THE BROADVIEW HOTEL

25 PLACES
TO SLEEP

———

5

BUDGET HOTELS

for the thrifty traveller

411 **HI TORONTO**
76 Church St
Downtown ①
+1 416 971 4440
hihostels.ca/en/
destinations/ontario/
hi-toronto

This hostel is clean, comfortable and located down in the heart of Toronto. Public transit is right nearby, and there is a bar inside where you can meet other travellers. HI organizes trips to different city highlights. The only available parking is in public lots nearby.

412 **TWO PEAS POD HOSTEL**
403 Spadina Avenue
Downtown ①
+1 416 217 1088
twopeas.me

Located in Chinatown, this is another hostel right in the middle of the city. The dorms are interesting. Each bed is a pod. It's more private than a regular bunk bed, and each bed comes equipped with a charging station and TV. Two Peas is a high-tech hostel.

413 **THE ONLY BACKPACKERS INN**
966 Danforth Ave
East York ④
+1 416 463 3249
the-only-backpackers-inn.com

This place feels like a true backpacker hostel. The bunks are creaky when you climb the ladder, and the bathrooms are shared. They do have some private rooms as well, with comfy queen beds. There's lots of funky artwork on the walls, and they have a nice patio.

414 THE PLANET TRAVELER

357 College St
Downtown ⓘ
+1 647 352 8747
theplanettraveler.com

This is an eco-friendly hostel that prides itself on using green energy. The hostel is bright and welcoming, with lots of large windows throughout. It's located on College Street so access to public transit is very convenient for visiting most tourist sites within Toronto. They have a nice rooftop patio for summer nights.

415 COLLEGE BACKPACKERS INN

280 Augusta Avenue
Downtown ⓘ
+1 416 929 4777
collegebackpackers.ca

College Backpackers Inn is a nicely renovated modern hostel in Kensington Market. The dorms are bright and clean. There's a free breakfast served each morning. But you probably won't eat in when staying here as there are so many awesome restaurants located nearby.

412 TWO PEAS POD HOSTEL

The 5 poshest
BOUTIQUE HOTELS
in the GTA

---

416 GLADSTONE HOTEL

1214 Queen St W
West End ⑥
+1 416 531 4635 xo
gladstonehotel.com

The Gladstone Hotel is Toronto's oldest operating hotel. It's a grand old building with a unique modern vibe in the creative centre of Toronto. Their focus is on art. Each of the rooms has been individually designed by an artist. They have three galleries in the hotel with rotating exhibits.

417 THE ANNEX

296 Brunswick Ave
Downtown ①
+1 647 694 9868
theannex.com

The Annex prides itself on being a comfortable boutique hotel. They've removed some typical hotel amenities in order to stay affordable. There is no front desk: if you need anything, you can reach the staff via text message. The hotel is situated in a 100-year-old building without an elevator. The rooms are bright and comfortable, and each room is equipped with an iPad and fast free Wi-Fi. The cafe downstairs serves awesome snacks and they are meticulous when it comes to making cocktails.

418 THE BROADVIEW HOTEL

106 Broadview Ave
East End ⑤
+1 416 362 8439
thebroadviewhotel.ca

The Broadview is another renovated historical building. The exterior has lovely arched windows. Many of the rooms have access to a terrace where you can relax or view the city from the east end. They have an amazing restaurant and a beautiful rooftop patio for summer nights.

419 THE ANNDORE HOUSE

15 Charles St E
Downtown ①
+1 833 745 8370
theanndorehouse.com

This is the ideal spot to stay if you're looking to be in the thick of things. It's just a stepping stone away from Yonge and Bloor. There are great shopping venues and restaurants nearby. The Anndore feels like an apartment building because it used to be one, but it's very comfortable and modern.

420 BISHA HOTEL

80 Blue Jays Way
Downtown ①
+1 877 270 0150
bishahoteltoronto.com

Bisha Hotel is located in the heart of Toronto's tourist district. It is just a few steps away from the CN Tower and the Rogers Centre. The poshest rooms offer a prime view of the city skyline and the lake. Rooms are large, spacious and decorated with a bold modern flair. They have several restaurants on-site. The Beachhouse Breakfast is delicious.

5
SPA HOTELS
near or in Toronto

421 **FOUR SEASONS HOTEL TORONTO**
60 Yorkville Avenue
Midtown ③
+1 416 964 0411
fourseasons.com/
toronto/spa

The Four Seasons is a nice hotel located close to a great shopping district. The spa is very professional and offers a variety of services. You can also go there for traditional Chinese medicine practices like cupping and gua sha. They even offer psychic services, which is pretty unique for a spa. Book a session and get all your questions answered.

424 MILLCROFT INN & SPA

422 INN ON THE TWENTY

3845 Main St
Jordan ⑩
ON L0R 1S0
+1 905 562 5336
innonthetwenty.com

Inn On The Twenty is a posh luxury hotel and is located in the historic Jordan village. There are 28 rooms and each room comes with a fireplace and a very comfortable seating area. The spa is elegant and provides a wide variety of services, like a wine country facial.

423 MIRAJ HAMMAM SPA – SHANGRI-LA

188 University Ave,
5th Floor
Downtown ①
+1 647 253 5770
mirajcaudaliespa.com

Inside the Shangri-La Hotel, the Miraj Spa offers a variety of services, including traditional Turkish spa services. It's an exotic experience in the middle of Toronto. The hammam is hot, steamy, and intense. They offer a full-body exfoliation service that uses the heat from the hammam, creating an invigorating experience.

424 MILLCROFT INN & SPA

55 John St
Alton ⑪
ON L7K 0C4
+1 519 941 8111
vintage-hotels.com/
millcroft

The Millcroft is located in the village of Alton. The area is picturesque with lots of old limestone buildings. Enjoy both spa services and the serenity of the hotel grounds. The restaurant is a well-respected fine dining establishment that features local artists as a part of the decor.

425 WHITE OAKS RESORT & SPA

253 Taylor Road SS4
Niagara-on-the-Lake ⑩
ON L0S 1J0
+1 800 263 5766
whiteoaksresort.com

White Oaks is a little more commercial in feel than other spas listed, but the services are comprehensive and high quality. They offer treatments like micro-dermabrasion and needling. The location is also excellent. You are close to a ton of wineries, the falls and bike paths along the river.

The 5 most convenient
CAMPGROUNDS
if you're visiting the GTA

---

426 GLEN ROUGE CAMPGROUND

7450 Kingston Road
Scarborough ⑦
ON M1B 0B7
+1 416 661 6600
trca.ca/parks/glen-
rouge-campground

The Rouge Park is our first National Urban Park. The Rouge Valley runs down the east side of the city, right in the middle of all the urban chaos. Glen Rouge – Toronto's only campground – contains all the typical amenities of a campground. They have oTENTiks, which are fancy tents best described using the term 'glamping'.

427 BRONTE CREEK

3201 Upper Middle
Road W
(off Bronte Road)
Oakville ⑨
ON L6M 4J7
+1 905 827 3228
ontarioparks.com/
park/brontecreek

Located in Oakville, this is a popular destination for fishermen who arrive for the yearly salmon run up the creek. It can get very busy. You won't feel like you're alone with nature at this location, but it is very convenient.

428 DARLINGTON PROVINCIAL PARK

1600 Darlington
Park Road
Bowmanville
ON L1C 3K3
+1 905 436 2036
ontarioparks.com/
park/darlington

Located further out of the city and to the east, this is a very pretty park located on the shores of Lake Ontario. It's very close to the nuclear plant but still beautiful, and the water is fairly warm here. The beach is very long and sandy.

429 SIBBALD POINT PROVINCIAL PARK

26071 Park Road
Jackson's Point ⓘ
ON L0E 1L0
+1 905 722 8061
ontarioparks.com/
park/sibbaldpoint

A short drive north of Toronto on Lake Simcoe, this is an easily accessible park that feels a little more in touch with nature. The beach is man-made but nice. They offer a variety of children's programming. It's also a good spot to bring a sailboat.

430 SANDBANKS PROVINCIAL PARK

3004 County Road 12
Picton
ON K0K 2T0
+1 613 393 3319
ontarioparks.com/
park/sandbanks

Sandbanks is a big park that draws both families and younger people who come to party with friends. The beach is amazing and great for little ones with its warm shallow waters. The dunes are the largest of their kind in the world. A 2-kilometre hike will take you through this unique habitat. It's an awesome thing to see.

5 **AREAS**

in which to rent an Airbnb

---

431 **MOSS PARK**

Queen St E going
north to Shuter St;
Sherbourne St going
west to Jarvis St
Downtown ①

This is not the fanciest of Toronto
neighbourhoods. Some of the buildings
are run-down. You might witness
an illicit transaction, but the people
are friendly, and you won't feel unsafe
walking down the street. The price for
an Airbnb is reasonable because of the
neighbourhood's reputation.

432 **RONCESVALLES VILLAGE**

Around Ronces-
valles Avenue
West End ⑥
roncesvallesvillage.ca

Roncesvalles is a more family-oriented
area. There are loads of restaurants in this
area. It has a nostalgic feel to it, and locals
tend to remember the 1960s with great
fondness. The shopping along 'Roncy'
Avenue is great. High Park is close by,
with lots of space for kids.

433 **HARBOURFRONT**

South of the
Gardiner Expressway;
East to Jarvis St
Downtown ②

Anything along the water will be
awesome. Harbourfront is close to main
attractions like the CN Tower, and it's
easy to access transit from here so you
can reach destinations outside the core.
It's pricey though, so be prepared to open
your wallet wide.

434 **PORT CREDIT**

The corridor along
Lakeshore Road W
Mississauga ⑧

Port Credit is the high-income neighbourhood of Mississauga. The western end is
Brueckner Rhododendron Gardens and
the eastern border is Seneca Avenue.
There are lots of boutiques here, along
with beautiful parks along the lakefront.
The area is much calmer and less noisy
than the rush of downtown. The city is
easily accessed by the Go Train.

435 **CLIFFCREST**

South of Eglinton
to the lake;
Kennedy Road east
to Bellamy Road
Scarborough ⑦

Cliffcrest is located in Scarborough. The
neighbourhood is named for its proximity
to the Scarborough Bluffs. You can spend
the day in the heart of the city and
then use transit to return to a quieter
neighbourhood and head to the beach at
Bluffer's Park in the evening. Remember
the beach is beautiful during the summer
months, but swimming after early
October is not recommended.

432 **RONCESVALLES VILLAGE**

BRUCE PENINSULA

30 PLACES TO HANG OUT ON WEEKENDS

---

5 beautiful **DRIVES**
around the **GTA**

---

436 **BELFOUNTAIN TO HOCKLEY VALLEY**
goo.gl/maps/
vDc821HTeWD7kzyR6
visitcaledon.ca/en/
tourism/belfountain.asp

Caledon, Ontario, is home to a UNESCO world biosphere reserve. The route from Belfountain to Hockley takes you through some beautiful scenery but also through some environmentally fragile lands. The Niagara Escarpment runs through this area, creating some amazing spots to hike on the Bruce Trail.

437 **SNAKE ROAD**
Hamilton ⑨
goo.gl/maps/
VaJcQZkR38mnJMd26

The Niagara Escarpment runs right through the middle of Hamilton. It has some beautiful waterfalls and makes for some lovely drives. There are lots of twisting and turning roads to be found in this area. During fall, when the leaves are changing, these roads turn into something magical.

438 **RIDGE ROAD**
goo.gl/maps/
8ZqLc2jpsnoJdJJn8

Along the southern shore of Lake Ontario, the Escarpment looms like a giant cliff running towards Niagara Falls. Ridge Road runs along the top of the escarpment and travels parallel to the highway but is a slower winding way of travel. You pass through wine country while on this road.

439 NEWCASTLE TO SHELTER VALLEY

goo.gl/maps/ QKDtm15cDH7d01z29

This route explores the lakeshore east of Toronto. Starting in Newcastle, you'll meander along roads that let you explore the small towns hidden away from the 401, which runs parallel and slightly to the north of this route. The town of Coburg is a good place to stop for lunch.

440 DOWNTOWN TORONTO TO NEWMARKET VIA YONGE ST

Yonge and Front St to Upper Canada Mall in Newmarket

This is an easy route, but be prepared for traffic. The route will take you through the centre of the city and up into the suburbs. There's a myth saying it's the longest road in the world. Perspective is everything: Yonge Street turns into Highway 11 and extends for 1800 kilometres north.

437 SNAKE ROAD

The 5 sweetest

MAPLE SYRUP FESTIVALS

---

441 MOUNTSBERG CONSERVATION AREA

2259 Milburough Line
Campbellville ⑨
ON L0P 1B0
+1 905 854 2276
conservationhalton. ca/
park-details?park=
mountsberg

Mountsberg is a large conservation area that boasts a petting zoo, a birds-of-prey exhibit, a large pond for fishing, hiking trails and of course, in spring, a maple syrup festival. They provide informative programming that will teach you all the ins and outs of maple syrup production.

442 KORTRIGHT CENTRE

9550 Pine Valley Dr
Woodbridge ⑪
ON L4L 1A6
+1 416 667 6295
kortright.org

This centre is just a quick trip north of the city. The Kortright Centre hosts a maple syrup festival each spring. They offer children's programming, including summer camps. The centre also offers programs for adults. It's a beautiful spot for a hike with 16 kilometres of open trails.

443 TERRA COTTA CONSERVATION AREA

14452 Winston
Churchill Boulevard
Terra Cotta ⑪
L7G 0N9
+1 905 877 1120
*cvc.ca/enjoy-the-outdoors/
conservation-areas*

Terra Cotta is another spot that allows you to explore the Niagara Escarpment. Their festival includes a fun informative booklet for kids to use when exploring the sugar bush. The pond also delights little ones and ducks swim around serenely, searching for food.

443 TERRA COTTA CONSERVATION AREA

444 PURPLE WOODS CONSERVATION AREA

38 Coates Road E
Oshawa
ON L1H 7K4
+1 905 579 0411
cloca.com/purple-woods-ca

In spring, local families flock to Purple Woods for their yearly festival. Little ones get a chance to see the syrup being produced and to try traditional tapping methods. You can sample maple sap as well as take home some of the syrup made on-site.

445 MAPLE MAGIC MISSISSAUGA

1620 Orr Road
Mississauga ⑧
ON L5J 4T2
+1 905 615 4860
culture.mississauga.ca/museums

Maple Magic is held at the Bradley Museum in Mississauga. The museum is a historic building that's open all year round. The festival includes local performers, children's activities and a chance to sample maple syrup. Try the maple taffy; it's a sticky treat made with syrup and snow.

5 cool places to try
ICE SKATING
outdoors

---

446 **NATHAN PHILLIPS SQUARE**
100 Queen St W
Downtown ①
toronto.ca

Skating in Nathan Phillips Square is just one of those things you need to do. It's a beautiful spot in the city. At night, the Toronto sign illuminates the square and vendors set up nearby so you can buy warm goodies after you've finished your time on the ice.

447 **COLONEL SAMUEL SMITH SKATING TRAIL**
AT: COLONEL SAMUEL SMITH PARK
65 Colonel Samuel Smith Park Road
Etobicoke ⑧
toronto.ca

This trail passes by the recreation centre, which is a converted power plant. You will find changing rooms inside. They use the walking paths as the base for creating the skating route through the southern area of the park. It's a fun route that takes you past some pretty scenery. The ice is always in good shape as they use a Zamboni for grooming.

448 NATREL RINK

AT: HARBOURFRONT
CENTRE
235 Queens Quay W
Downtown ②
+1 416 954 9866
harbourfrontcentre.com/
venues/natrelrink

Skating downtown at Harbourfront Centre is a fun experience. You can zoom around the rink while enjoying a view of the lake. They offer skate rentals as well as lessons for children and adults. The rink opens in November. Check the website for details on DJ skate nights.

449 GRENADIER POND

AT: HIGH PARK
200 Park Side Drive
West End ⑥
cityrinks.ca

Grenadier Pond is a beautiful spot to skate. Many take advantage of the cold weather and enjoy time on the pond. The city has suspended its ice-monitoring operation, and no longer advises the public about ice safety, so skating here is at your own risk. High Park also offers a second skating location, at the outdoor swimming pool. Or you can visit the ice rink at Rennie Park which is right across the pond.

450 THE BENTWAY SKATE TRAIL

AT: FORT YORK
250 Fort York Blvd
Downtown ②
+1 416 304 0222
thebentway.ca

The Bentway is a unique spot in Toronto. Located under the Gardiner Expressway, the space offers a variety of programs during the winter and summer. You can skate and enjoy DJ nights here during the winter. They also promote the work of local artists on the pillars of the highway.

5 weekend trips
OUT OF THE GTA

---

451 KILLBEAR PROVINCIAL PARK

35 Killbear Park Rd
Nobel
ON P0G 1G0
+1 705 342 5492
ontarioparks.com/park/killbear

This is one of the most beautiful parks in Ontario. It's wild, rugged and easily accessible from the city. The beach is sandy and spacious, but the water is cold. Bring your camping gear but heed park warnings about bears. There are lots in the area. We keep our parks wild in Canada.

452 ELORA GORGE

7400 Wellington
County Road 21
Elora
ON N0B 1S0
+1 519 846 9742
grandriver.ca/en/outdoor-recreation/Elora-Gorge.aspx

The waters of Elora Gorge are a beautiful turquoise that will remind you of the Caribbean, with the difference being the water temperature. Let's call this an invigorating Canadian swimming experience. It's a perfect spot for a dip on a hot day. You can also go tubing on the river or take a stroll through Elora. The town has lots of beautiful shops, many of which sell local artisan work.

453 THOUSAND ISLANDS

visit1000islands.com
brockville.com

A trip to the Thousand Islands will place you right in the middle of the weekend holiday terrain for Torontonians. Brockville and the surrounding area host thousands of visitors each summer. A boat tour of the islands is a highlight. You can also book a kayaking tour through the area.

454 SOUTHAMPTON AND THE BRUCE PENINSULA

Saugeen Shores ⑪
visitsouthampton.ca

Southampton is far quieter than nearby Sauble Beach, and just as nice. There's a boardwalk for evening strolls along the lakeshore, and on Thursdays a piper plays at the flagpole during sunset. It's also a great base for exploring the Bruce Peninsula. There is tonnes of hiking in this area.

455 COLLINGWOOD

Clearview
Simcoe County ⑪
collingwood.ca

Collingwood draws local holiday goers year-round. In winter there's a ski hill with a view over Georgian Bay. The Blue Mountains hills aren't large, but they are beautiful. In summer you can swim, go hiking, visit the caves or go tree-top trekking. It's a busy spot, so prepare for crowds.

The 5 best resources for
PADDLING *in Toronto*

456 **HARBOURFRONT CANOE & KAYAK CENTRE**

283 Queens Quay W Downtown ②
+1 416 203 2277
paddletoronto.com

This is a comprehensive rental centre that offers both lessons and tours. They have several tours for beginners, including a 3-hour paddle tour around Toronto Islands. Think about trying a stand-up paddleboard. The bay area is a beautiful spot for a paddle in the evening.

457 **HUMBER RIVER KAYAKING & CANOEING**

AT: KING'S MILL PARK
2649 Bloor St W Etobicoke ⑧
ON M8X 0A5
+1 416 536 2067
torontoadventures.ca/ adventures/kayaking andcanoeing

The Humber River is wide, calm, and the perfect place for beginners to learn the ins and outs of paddling. Try out one of their guided night-time tours. The lights of Toronto reflect on the water and make for beautiful photographs. They also offer lessons and rentals.

458 THE COMPLETE PADDLER

919 Oxford St
Etobicoke ⑧
ON M8Z 5T3
+1 416 255 6905
completepaddler.ca

This is a large store located just south of the Gardiner Expressway. The staff are knowledgeable and helpful when you need to purchase or rent gear. They also offer paddling lessons, which are held in a local pool. You can even complete canoe certification courses with this establishment.

459 ROUGE NATIONAL URBAN PARK

Zoo Road (adjacent
to Toronto Zoo)
Scarborough ⑦
+1 416 264 2020
pc.gc.ca/en/pn-np/
on/rouge

You can paddle on the Rouge River through this new urban park. Parks Canada monitors the river and the trails within, but they don't offer any rentals or lessons. You can rent from one of the other vendors and have the items delivered to the Rouge location.

460 CENTRE ISLAND BOAT HOUSE

Toronto Islands
Downtown ②
torontoisland.com/
boathouse.php

If you're an absolute beginner but don't want to take lessons, the lagoon on Centre Island is a good place to try paddling. It's calm, fairly shallow, and there's lots of wildlife to watch as you paddle through. Centre Island also rents out canoes, kayaks and pedal boats.

5 of the best hikes on the
BRUCE TRAIL

461 BRUCE PENINSULA

*goo.gl/maps/
Wh7R6yiyF8x5g5ii9,
pc.gc.ca/en/pn-np/
on/bruce/activ/
experiences/sentiers-
trails*

The 3-hour drive up to Bruce Peninsula NP is worth it. The challenging hike from halfway Log Dump to the Grotto offers incredible views of Georgian Bay, along with several great spots for swimming. The trail requires good shoes and being in good shape. Book your entrance to the park online weeks in advance, as it gets busy in summer.

461 BRUCE PENINSULA

462 BOYNE VALLEY
PARKING AT:
19 County Road
Mulmur ⑪
ontariotrails.on.ca

Walking the Primrose Loop in Boyne Valley feels like walking through a fairy forest. If you visit, you will understand why: in early summer the moss will remind you of a fantasy movie. There are lots of crevices to explore off the main trail; just be careful, it's easy to slip.

463 SHORT HILLS PROVINCIAL PARK
PARKING AT:
Pelham Road
Thorold ⑩
ontariotrails.on.ca

The southern part of the Niagara Region offers a milder climate than that north of Toronto. This allows for the growth of the Carolinian forest. This type of forest is quite rare in Ontario.

464 LIMEHOUSE & SPEYSIDE
PARKING AT:
12169 Fifth Line
Limehouse ⑪
ON L0P 1H0
ontariotrails.on.ca

The trails in this area offer hikers a chance to experience a little bit of adventurous hiking. There are some very steep parts that require you to climb and descend ladders. It's best to attempt this trail with children over the age of 7.

465 BEAVER VALLEY – EUGENIA FALLS
Grey Highlands ⑪
ON N0C 1E0
ontariotrails.on.ca

This trail in Eugenia offers several opportunities to explore. If you are adventurous, follow the trail to the bottom of the gorge, then follow the riverbed up to the waterfall. In summer the water levels are low, and you can stand at the bottom of the falls.

INFO:
brucetrail.org

VIEW FROM CN TOWER

35 RANDOM FACTS

5 facts about **CANADIAN INDIGENOUS CULTURE**

466 JUNE 21ST IS NATIONAL INDIGENOUS PEOPLES DAY

Sadly, in the past indigenous groups in Canada were often mistreated. Indigenous culture is steadily growing, and National Indigenous Peoples Day is an opportunity to celebrate that. An online search will easily bring up many events you are welcome to attend on this day.

467 RECONCILIATION IS IMPORTANT

As Canada tries to repair its relationship with its indigenous peoples, you will find that many events and the Canadian news will be filled with information about reconciliation. The idea is to bring awareness to the past and move forward positively.

468 INDIGENOUS PEOPLES ARE STILL A DISTINCT GROUP

Indigenous people are still alive and well today. The images of people in feathers, beads and living in teepees are only part of the story. Check out these creative individuals to find out more: Iskwē, A Tribe Called Red and Alanis Obomsawin.

469 POW WOWS ARE FOR EVERYONE

Pow wows are public events. They are a weekend-long celebration of indigenous culture. Individuals compete in different dances. You'll find great food, amazing regalia and families proudly sharing their culture with anyone who wishes to visit.

470 TORONTO IS AN INDIGENOUS WORD

Many city names are derived from indigenous words. Toronto and Ottawa both originate from indigenous languages. Toronto is from the Mohawk language. It means 'where there are trees in water'. The original word was *Tkaronto*.

The 5 most obvious
D I F F E R E N C E S between
Canada and the **U S A**

471 WE HAVE A PRIME MINISTER

The leader of Canada is referred to as the Prime Minister, while the Americans have a president. Canada is also a part of the Commonwealth. The Queen of England is still considered the head of state, even if it is only a formality.

472 OUR MONEY IS COLOURFUL

Our dollar bills are all classified by colour. When you open your wallet, you'll discover a rainbow. 5 dollar bills are blue, 10 dollar bills are purple, 20 dollar bills are green. American money is all the same colour, a darker green.

473 WE DON'T LIKE TO BE CALLED AMERICANS

Canadians are just as proud of their country as Americans are. We're just not as loud about it. One of the things that tend to frustrate us Canadians is when others assume we are American. There is a difference, and we all want you to be aware of it.

474 WE HAVE UNIVERSAL HEALTHCARE

Tommy Douglas, the grandfather of actor Kiefer Sutherland, was a politician and the man credited with championing universal healthcare. Our system provides care to all, regardless of insurance or the ability to pay. It's not a perfect system, but it differs greatly from the USA.

475 IT'S EXPENSIVE TO FLY ACROSS CANADA

For whatever economic reason, it's just as expensive to fly across Canada as it is to fly from Toronto to Europe. Many Torontonians will drive to cities like Buffalo in the US to take advantage of cheaper flights to e.g. Vancouver.

472 OUR MONEY IS COLOURFUL

5 facts about the
LEGALIZATION
OF MARIJUANA *in Canada*

---

476 THE PURCHASE OF MARIJUANA WAS FIRST MADE LEGAL IN CANADA ON OCTOBER 17, 2018

When it was first legalized, you had to order your pot through a website and parcels were shipped using Canada Post. Post offices were often filled with boxes of pot awaiting pickup.

477 BRICKS-AND-MORTAR STORES ARE SCARCE

There are a lot of regulations surrounding the bricks-and-mortar stores selling marijuana. There was a lot of concern about the location of the stores and their proximity to children. Slowly, stores are beginning to appear in neighbourhoods.

478 YOU CANNOT SMOKE IN PUBLIC

Marijuana falls under the same rules as alcohol. You cannot smoke it in public. There are strict laws about drinking and driving and marijuana use carries the same penalty. You are expected to smoke only in private places and to consume responsibly.

479 YOU MUST BE 19 YEARS OF AGE TO PURCHASE

Cigarette use and alcohol use are highly regulated in Canada and marijuana falls under the same laws. You will be asked to show identification. There are many signs informing patrons that ID is checked if you look 30 years old or younger. Don't be insulted, just go with the flow. Sometimes Canadians can be very precise, so be prepared.

480 THE GOVERNMENT REGULATES SALES

The Canadian government tracks sales and collects taxes from the sale of marijuana. The product is highly regulated. Prices tend to be high, and the boxes clearly outline the content of each brand of marijuana.

STORE SELLING MARIJUANA.

The 5 most important things
to know about CANADIAN WINTERS

---

481 WE HAVE SKI HILLS, BUT THEY'RE NOT LIKE B.C.

There are many ski slopes close to Toronto, but if you have skied in places like British Columbia, you will be disappointed. One of the nicest hills is at Blue Mountain in Collingwood. Many Ontarians travel to Quebec to ski during the winter. This may be an option for you.

482 THE REST OF THE COUNTRY MAKES FUN OF TORONTO'S WINTERS

Winters in Toronto are pretty severe compared to European standards. Temperatures average around -10 degrees Celsius during the winter months. The Great Lakes regulate temperatures in southern Ontario, keeping them fairly mild by Canadian standards. The rest of the country laughs when Torontonians complain about cold weather.

483 IT'S COLD, BUT EMBRACE IT!

Winters in Canada are cold. Many will tell you to avoid coming here during the winter. If you do choose to visit during the winter, you'll love it. Embrace the cold! Dress well and try some of our favourite winter activities. Skating outdoors at night, followed by wine in front of the fireplace makes for an incredible evening.

484 THE ICE IS DANGEROUS

Winter is amazing, but you also have to take your safety into consideration. Always watch out for ice on sidewalks or while driving. Black ice is the worst; you can't see it. Ask for advice from locals before driving during winter storms. It can be nerve-wracking for even the most experienced Canadians.

485 MARCH AND APRIL ARE UNPREDICTABLE

During March and April, you never know what kind of weather you might face. You could experience a beautiful sunny spring day. You could also run into a violent springtime snowstorm. If visiting during these months, be prepared for anything.

5 IMPORTANT THINGS *to know about the* GTA

---

486 TORONTO IS NOT A LARGE CITY

The city of Toronto has a total population of around 3 million people. The GTA raises that total to somewhere around 5 million people. Don't let the small number fool you. The city is very spread out. Distances in Canada are far greater than in Europe, for example.

487 THE PUBLIC TRANSIT ISN'T VERY EXTENSIVE

In the downtown core and along the main GO train line, it's very easy to take public transit. Unfortunately, Toronto lacks a good system that extends out into the suburbs and smaller surrounding towns. It is advisable to consider renting a car if leaving the GTA. Even for a trip to Niagara wine country.

488 IT IS ONE OF THE MOST MULTICULTURAL CITIES IN THE WORLD

Unless you are an indigenous person, your family came from somewhere else. Toronto prides itself on being a multicultural mosaic. You're just as likely to walk down the street and hear Mandarin or Hindi as you are to hear English.

489 URBAN SPRAWL IS AN ISSUE

Toronto takes up a lot of space and the suburbs even more so. Urban sprawl is a major issue in Ontario. As cities expand, they are taking up farmland, and the lack of good transit often creates heavy traffic. Highway 401 is huge. In some spots there are 22 lanes to navigate through.

490 MOST PEOPLE LIVE IN THE SOUTH

The majority of the population in Ontario lives around the Great Lakes, close to the 49th parallel. If you choose to leave the city and head north, you will find that cities get smaller quickly. Our most northern towns will only have a few hundred residents.

The 5 **STEREOTYPES**
Canadians love to embrace

491 WE'RE INCREDIBLY POLITE

youtube.com/watch? v=RR5rIv4Qros

As a whole, Canadians are very careful not to hurt anyone's feelings. There are tons of jokes out there about how many times we will say "sorry". It's a habit, and we will happily make fun of ourselves. It's part of being Canadian.

492 ALL WE THINK ABOUT IS HOCKEY

Hockey is huge in Canada. For years, *Hockey Night* in Canada was the only show people watched on Saturday nights. We're proud of our hockey teams. You will find skit after skit on comedy shows making fun of our obsession. The truth is, however, we also love our basketball. Go Raptors!

493 WE ALL WEAR PLAID

youtube.com/watch? v=ssCZWBtwUTI

The famous Canadian comedy sketch of Bob and Doug McKenzie covers just about every Canadian stereotype out there. These are classic Canadian skits, check them out! We're proud.

494 BEER IS ALL WE DRINK

Canadians love their beer. We pride ourselves on its quality. There are many jokes about how superior Canadian beer is in comparison to American beer. All stereotypes aside, we also make some amazing wines, ciders and our Canadian cocktail, the Caesar, is awesome.

495 WE SAY "EH" WAY TOO MUCH

The interjection "eh" does creep into the Canadian vocabulary. I've been caught using it several times. It is part of our vernacular. However, sometimes we take it too far as a part of the joke, and you'll find lots of skits where "eh" creeps into conversation a ton of times.

492 ALL WE THINK ABOUT IS HOCKEY

5 **HOLIDAYS**

that are unique to Canada

---

496 CANADA DAY

July 1st is Canada Day. This is the day when we celebrate the creation of the country. You'll find lots of different celebrations occurring throughout the city. The best place to watch the fireworks is at the bottom of the CN Tower.

497 VICTORIA DAY WEEKEND

Celebrated on the third weekend of May, this holiday honours the birthday of Queen Victoria. In reality, it's a fun long weekend to mark the beginning of the summer season. Many Torontonians will head north to cottage country at this time.

498 LABOUR DAY WEEKEND

The US also celebrates this holiday. This is the last long weekend of the summer. Kids head back to school right after this holiday, and many families use it as a time to celebrate before the weather turns cold.

499 **AUGUST CIVIC HOLIDAY**

The civic holiday was created so that there was one long weekend in each month of summer. Many summer festivals are held on this weekend, so you'll find lots to do. Just be aware most stores will remain closed on the Monday of the long weekend.

500 **FAMILY DAY WEEKEND**

Family Day was created approximately ten years ago. Ontario celebrates Family Day on the third Monday of February. It was created to give folks a break during the long dark days of winter. Not all businesses recognize Family Day, but many community events are scheduled on this day.

INDEX

COLOPHON

EDITING, COMPOSING *and* PHOTOGRAPHY — Erin FitzGibbon —
www.erinfitzgibbon.com

GRAPHIC DESIGN — Joke Gossé and Sarah Schrauwen

COVER IMAGE — The Bentway (secret 450)

The addresses in this book have been selected after thorough independent
research by the author, in collaboration with Luster Publishing. The selection
is solely based on personal evaluation of the business by the author. Nothing
in this book was published in exchange for payment or benefits of any kind.

D/2020/12.005/1

ISBN 978 94 6058 2622

NUR 513, 510

© 2020 Luster, Antwerp
www.lusterweb.com — WWW.THE500HIDDENSECRETS.COM
info@lusterweb.com

Printed in Italy by Printer Trento.

MIX
Paper from
responsible sources
FSC® C015829

All rights reserved.
No part of this publication may be reproduced,
stored in a retrieval system, or transmitted, in any
form or by any means, without the prior written
consent of the publisher. An exception is made
for short excerpts, which may be cited for the sole
purpose of reviews.